A YEAR OF
MINDFULNESS FOR BEGINNERS

A YEAR OF

Mindfulness

FOR BEGINNERS

DAILY MANTRAS, MEDITATIONS, AND PROMPTS

LEE PAPA

ROCKRIDGE PRESS

For general information on our other products and services or to obtain technical support, please contact our Customer Care Department within the United States at (866) 744-2665, or outside the United States at (510) 253-0500.

Rockridge Press publishes its books in a variety of electronic and print formats. Some content that appears in print may not be available in electronic books, and vice versa.

Interior and Cover Designer: Jill Lee

Art Producer: Karen Williams

Editor: Emily Angell and Claire Yee

Production Manager: Riley Hoffman

Production Editor: Melissa Edeburn

Illustration © Amanda Leon, p 44.

Author photo courtesy of © Jerry Metellus.

ISBN: Print 978-1-64152-848-1 | eBook 978-1-64152-849-8

R0

To the Principle Substance in which all knowledge and wisdom is generated and all motion is celebrated.

Contents

Mindfulness equals awareness: awareness of your thoughts and actions and the world around you—without judgment.

—LEE PAPA

Introduction

A friend once remarked that I had a lot of self-help books. I found that humorous because I had not perceived the books that way. My intention was to know myself by understanding my patterns; breaking through my limits; exploring my consciousness; poking around my emotions; delving into my beliefs; investigating my ego; and understanding death, relationships, and love. I wanted to look at trauma and drama, seek out ancient knowledge, explore the mind-body-spirit connection, and ease my own emotional suffering. I'm excited to share my years of acquired experiential and educational knowledge with you.

Through mindfulness, I have questioned beliefs that held me locked in a less-than-optimal version of myself. I was filled with stress, fears, illness, programmed thinking, and reactionary emotional triggers. I look back on that younger me with compassion. It was exhausting being that person. I recall that when I encountered challenges, I would search for a miraculous solution that would help me make sense of what was happening in my life and the world around me. Then, a near-death experience awakened me to the nature of reality: love, knowledge, and wisdom. I understood that my chaos and illness yielded wisdom, and I adopted a mindfulness practice.

In 2009, I opened a wellness center in Las Vegas, Nevada. It facilitated some 4,000 classes on meditation, Reiki, and yoga, and it served more than 10,000 attendees seeking relief from suffering in its various forms—anxiety, sleeplessness, lack of self-confidence, poor body image, depression, shame, addiction. Many attendees wished to liberate themselves from their emotional turmoil, and mindfulness practices supported them.

Nowadays, *mindfulness* is a widely used term and a widely misunderstood concept. Is it meditation? Is it yoga? Let's clear up a couple of things: Some people engage in mindfulness-based meditations, and meditation is certainly a part of mindfulness, but mindfulness encompasses much more. Mindfulness is part of every decision. It is a philosophy of life. Mindfulness is the nonjudgmental awareness of your thoughts, actions, and the world around you.

Mindfulness is a lifelong practice.

This book is a road map to the daily mindfulness practice that led me and others to a life of peace and joy. This practice does not replace your faith. It deepens your faith.

It may be hard to believe that a daily mindfulness practice can motivate you or expand your state of awareness. But once you acknowledge the power of your intention and take responsibility for your own well-being, you'll see how powerful mindfulness can be. Small daily changes lead to big improvements.

This book will assist you in your mindfulness practice. It is filled with inspiring quotes, awareness-expanding exercises and meditations, prompts for contemplation and journaling, and affirmations. When presented with an affirmation, repeat it throughout the day—or longer if it really resonates with you. If a daily entry doesn't resonate with you, skip to one that does.

Mindfulness is one of the most profound gifts you can offer yourself. Give it priority and understand that mindfulness is called a "practice" for a reason. It is not something to be achieved or conquered.

Although mindfulness is an extraordinarily effective way to meet challenges, it is not a replacement for therapeutic treatment. There is no weakness or shame in seeking help. Rather, it's empowering to take responsibility for your well-being, and this book will support you on that path.

When you understand intimately that your human life experience has ebbs and flows like that of the ocean, that both the ups and downs are to be honored, you will achieve peace. Remember, mindfulness is awareness without judgment, and who do we tend to judge the most? Ourselves! So, as you begin reading this book, establish your intention to honor yourself every day with acceptance and joy. I believe in you, and you will too!

JANUARY

1
JANUARY

An intention is not just a goal; it is the deeper meaning and feeling behind what you do. When used deliberately and for the highest good with joy, love, and/or appreciation, an intention is a powerful force that fuels the experience you seek. Sit quietly, close your eyes, and listen to your breath. Ask yourself, "What is my intention for my mindfulness journey?" Grab your notebook and write down your intention for this exciting first step into mindfulness practice.

2
JANUARY

Throughout the day, repeat to yourself, "I am not my mind. I am not my body. I am spirit—a nonphysical being using the mind and body as sacred tools for my journey."

3
JANUARY

~~~

Mirror, Mirror

You don't have to wait for a new year or a milestone birthday to start fresh. With each new day or moment, you are given an opportunity for renewal. Allow yourself to begin your journey of inner exploration. Stand in front of a mirror and take a few deep breaths, in through your nose and out through your mouth. Now, look at your reflection and say to yourself, "I give myself permission to have a mindful experience today and every day to reach my highest expression." Your highest expression is however you define the best version of yourself.

4
JANUARY

~~~

To find the secrets of the universe, think in terms of energy, frequency and vibration.

—NIKOLA TESLA

5
JANUARY

~~~

When you become mindfully aware of your intention behind a decision or action, you may realize that your objective is not optimal or deliberate. Instead, your intention may be coming from a habit of making decisions from a place of obligation, guilt, or a mentality of lack. In your notebook, write down the higher intentions you can hold for this day, conversation, meeting, or experience. Keep these higher intentions in mind as you proceed through your day.

6
JANUARY

~~~

During the beginning stages of your practice, repeat, "I am in the process of navigating my life mindfully with ease and grace." After a week or two, drop the words "in the process of," leaving you with the more affirmative statement: "I am navigating my life mindfully with ease and grace."

7

JANUARY

Mindful Breath

Use this exercise to relax your body. Sit comfortably in a chair with your feet flat on the ground and your hands resting in your lap. Keep your spine and neck straight. Close your eyes and breathe deeply in through your nose, hold for a count of three, and exhale through your mouth for a count of three. Deepen each breath by expanding your chest and belly with each inhale. Take three of these mindful breaths before returning to your natural breath. Continue to stay aware of your breath and notice how it feels moving through your nose, lungs, and mouth. (You can do this as a short meditation or before a longer meditation, if you wish.)

8

JANUARY

With the new day comes new strength and new thoughts.

—ELEANOR ROOSEVELT

9
JANUARY

~

Go Outside

It is easy to get lost in your various electronics as your only contact to the outside world. Today, take a 10-minute walk with no electronic barriers so that you can hear nature, smell the air, fill your lungs, look at the scenery, and find natural beauty. Even if you live in a congested city, focus your new awareness and notice natural beauty. Allow this awareness to bring a smile to your face.

10
JANUARY

~

Release the notion of "work-life balance." The teeter-totter of balance does not serve you. Instead, bring your awareness to creating an integration of life—in your personal and professional life as well as in the inner and outer world of your consciousness. Integrating all parts of your life and self through a mindfulness practice helps you flow with life with more ease and grace.

11
JANUARY

~~~

**The subconscious doesn't distinguish sarcasm and
jokes. It just accepts what it hears. That's the power
of words.**

—INDIA.ARIE

12
JANUARY

~~~

Are you aggravated in some aspect of your life? Much of the annoy-
ance we feel is a story we make up about a scenario that holds no
truth. We are so programmed for stress that we often create it where
none is needed. Today, be aware of when you are allowing your mind
to fabricate a story that does not serve you. Is this fabrication occurring
because of an old pattern of stress or lack of self-worth? Get your notebook and explore more of this process through some journaling.

13
JANUARY

~~~

Happiness is a butterfly which, when pursued is just beyond your grasp . . . but if you will sit down quietly, may alight upon you.

—NATHANIEL HAWTHORNE

14
JANUARY

~~~

Breath Awareness

As humans, we have become accustomed to panting our way through life. Today, be aware of your breath throughout the day. Set your phone alarm to gently chime each hour on the hour or as often as you like or feel is optimal to fully experience this exercise. When the alarm chimes, stop and take a deeper breath, envisioning the cleansing air of renewal revitalizing your body. Be sure to honor yourself. If you turn the alarm off without taking a few moments to become aware of your breath, you will not be honoring yourself, which holds an energy of self-betrayal. With your upcoming day in mind, be sure to set your alarm for realistic intervals.

15
JANUARY

~

A belief is only a thought you continue to think. A belief is nothing more than a chronic pattern of thought, and you have the ability—if you try even a little bit—to begin a new pattern, to tell a new story, to achieve a different vibration, to change your point of attraction.

—ABRAHAM HICKS

16
JANUARY

~

Make a list of the areas in which you're experiencing obstacles. Is there a pattern to the challenges you encounter, such as problematic relationships, money issues, or poor health? Bring your mindful, nonjudgmental awareness to your patterns of contrast (challenges or suffering). When you're focused on moving forward instead of evaluating the present based on the past, it can be difficult to notice these patterns, but when you recognize them, you can take steps to change the outcome through mindful awareness in the present.

17
JANUARY

~

Being aware of the duality in everything—light and dark, right and wrong, yin and yang—will lead you to knowing and accepting the unity, the oneness, of all. Throughout the day, repeat this affirmation: "No longer am I fixated on the perception of duality. I acknowledge and accept the unity and value of all experiences."

18
JANUARY

~

Be the hero in your own life! It's important to live with the intention that all experience provides valuable insight. Where have you played the victim in your past? Has being the victim served you, or has it hindered your well-being? Journal in your notebook and explore how the limiting pattern of playing the victim has shown itself in your life.

19
JANUARY

~~~

We could never learn to be brave and patient, if there were only joy in the world.

—HELEN KELLER

20
JANUARY

~~~

Cleansing Rain

Sit comfortably with your feet flat on the floor and close your eyes. Place all your awareness on your breath. Inhale through your nose and exhale through your mouth, allowing your mind to become still as you focus on your breath. If thoughts arise, allow them to subside as you return to the stillness. Continue to breathe in and breathe out. Now, envision yourself sitting on a large porch of a country house on a rainy day. The sound is soothing, and the cleansing rain has refreshed the air to the point that when you breathe in, you smell the renewal in the air. Breathe in the crisp, cool, fresh air for a minute, and then if you desire to, continue for another 5 to 10 minutes. Allow your breath to sink into the soothing sounds of the rain and let go of your thoughts by returning to your breath.

21
JANUARY

~~~

Knowing that you are in full control of your destiny allows a clear path to unfold. Say to yourself, "I am the deliberate creator of my reality."

22
JANUARY

~~~

The trio-of-transformation is the understanding of the mind, body, and spirit connection where your higher consciousness unfolds. (See the resources on page 220.) Many people focus on just one area of well-being and allow the other areas, such as the spiritual element, to atrophy. Some shy away from the spiritual element, but it is critical in the evolution of consciousness. It is the purpose behind the mind and body. Explore this question: Do you see yourself as mostly body, mind, or spirit? In your notebook, write down three things you can implement to develop the neglected areas.

23
JANUARY

~

Slideshow of Thoughts

Begin by sitting comfortably. Close your eyes, breathe in through your nose, and exhale through your mouth for a count of three, before allowing your breath to relax into its natural rhythm. If a thought arises, do not resist it or push it away. Tell yourself you'll remember the important thoughts later, when you need them. Allow your thoughts to move on by like a slideshow, and bring yourself back to the present.

Envision yourself standing under a magnificent cleansing waterfall that flows with the colors of the rainbow in rotation. In your imagination, experience each color washing over you as it cleanses your body of energies that no longer serve you: drama, pain, sorrow, limits, and patterns. Breathe in each color: violet, indigo, blue, green, yellow, orange, and red. Cleanse your body of unwanted energies and ready yourself for the day. (See the resources on page 220 to experience this as a guided meditation.)

24
JANUARY

~

Make this your mantra today: "I am perfect always and in all ways."

25
JANUARY

~~~

Move That Body

Sometimes, your energy may feel sluggish and stagnant and your body needs some mindful attention to get the energy flowing again. Today, honor yourself with five minutes of a song that gets you moving—you know, the song that you hear the first couple of beats of and instinctively want to turn up the volume and dance. Play that song and move! Dance and sing aloud. Be silly and smile. If it has been so long that you don't remember what song makes your body want to move, do an Internet search or peruse your music library. You can even create a go-to playlist that you can turn to anytime you want to elevate your energy with a little dance and movement to shake off the dust bunnies.

26
JANUARY

~~~

Today, turn to this affirmation for support: "I am creating the highest and best expression of myself today and every day."

27
JANUARY

Mindfulness and meditation are known as "a practice" for a reason. Mindfulness is not meant to be achieved, conquered, or overcome—in fact, it's the antithesis of that mindset. It is in the surrender to the moment-by-moment practice of mindfulness and meditation that our higher consciousness emerges and our emotions that cause suffering fade. In your notebook, journal about any times you spent too much energy attempting to conquer something that would have been better served by release or surrender. When have you surrendered, and how did that feel?

28
JANUARY

Feelings come and go like clouds in a windy sky. Conscious breathing is my anchor.

—THICH NHAT HANH

29

~~~

Listen to Your Body

Sit quietly and listen to your breath. Give thanks to your body for being the sacred vessel that holds your spirit. Now, listen with mindful attention to the cues from your body that you may have been too scattered to feel previously. Your body is a magnificent tool of resonance. With each decision that presents itself today, ask your body, "How does that feel? Does the opportunity feel light or heavy in my body?" As you continue to practice this awareness, it will get easier to know what feels light and what feels heavy, what is a yes and what is a no. If something feels light, act upon it. If something feels heavy, decline to engage it. Use this awareness to help with your decisions—whether for food intake, invitations, people you engage with, words you choose, and everything in between. Refrain from feeling judgment, whether good or bad; simply interpret your body's cues of lightness or heaviness, optimal or less than optimal. Know that your body's answer is for that moment and situation. It could change tomorrow.

30
JANUARY

Throughout the day, repeat this affirmation: "I am renewed, refreshed, and recharged."

31
JANUARY

In your notebook, reflect on the topic of happiness: How has happiness presented itself in your life? Do you seek it outside yourself? Is it that next vacation, the special edition purchase, or the must-have electronic that brings you happiness? How about celebrations, new jobs, special events, time with friends and family, television, celebrities, or the monthly membership box? Through your mindfulness practice, you will learn that happiness is not an external destination. It resides within you. When you honor yourself enough to open the door of inner exploration, you will tap into the deep well of lasting happiness. You'll no longer need to rely on the external to provide happiness for you. Happiness is an inside game!

FEBRUARY

1
FEBRUARY

The journey I'm taking is inside me. Just like blood travels down veins, what I'm seeing is my inner self and what seems threatening is just the echo of the fear in my heart.

—HARUKI MURAKAMI

2
FEBRUARY

To understand love, you must also explore fear. Though it may seem odd, love and fear are often confused in decision-making. Love is freedom, peace, and liberation. Fear holds you back from love. With any decision, ask yourself, "Is this decision based on fear or love?" If fear, ask yourself, "Where is the fear coming from?" Journal on this topic and work toward releasing your fear. (See the resources on page 220 for assistance with this prompt.)

We Are Frequency

Science tells us that everything is energy. In The Hidden Messages in Water by Masaru Emoto, and similar books, we learn that our words and our thoughts carry a frequency that creates an outcome. As we move through a mindfulness and/or consciousness-raising practice, the goal is to elevate our frequency. We do this through understanding our words, thoughts, and emotions. When we experience a situation that produces an emotion such as fear, our vibration takes a dip. The Map of Consciousness, pictured on page 22 and developed by Dr. David R. Hawkins, shows the energetic frequency associated with each emotion. Today, I invite you to be mindful of when you allow fear into your experience, and to play with choosing a love-based direction instead.

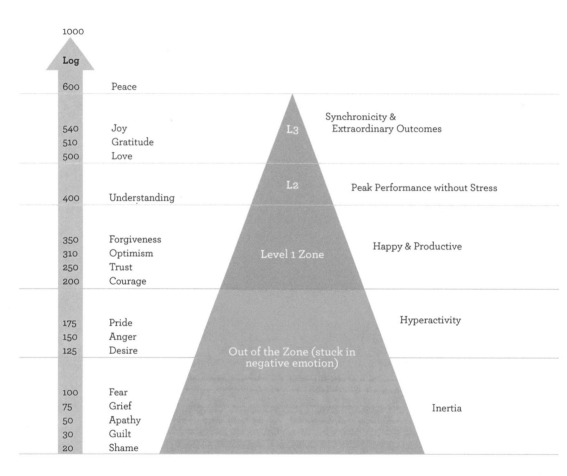

4
FEBRUARY

~

When a resolute young fellow steps up to the great bully, the world, and takes him boldly by the beard, he is often surprised to find it comes off in his hand, and that it was only tied on to scare away the timid adventurers.

—RALPH WALDO EMERSON

5
FEBRUARY

~

Make this your mantra today: "I love and approve of myself today and every day."

6
FEBRUARY

Self-love is a concept that makes many people feel uncomfortable or confused. Some people think having self-love is akin to being selfish. This notion keeps us small and not in our power. Self-love is not selfish at all. Write in your notebook and journal: "Self-love: the care and honoring of oneself as the individual expression of the sacred whole." (See the resources on page 220 to explore this topic.)

7
FEBRUARY

Self-Care

Do something nice for yourself today that doesn't cost anything. Whatever you choose to treat yourself, be sure that it doesn't involve any chores or work-related activities. Self-care is not selfish; it's mandatory for your optimal health and well-being.

8
FEBRUARY

~~~

When you go into the space of nothingness, everything becomes known.

—GAUTAMA BUDDHA

9
FEBRUARY

~~~

You are a spiritual warrior. You are a spiritual being with a physical experience on this planet, and you have blinders on about the reality of your existence. You have come into this world with preset codes, and your job is to break through these limits and uncover what is underneath. All your obstacles, dramas, traumas, sorrows, pains, and suffering are beautifully set up so that you can see the truth of who you are. This is true for all of us. In your notebook, journal your response to this question: "Who am I?" Don't overthink the question; allow the flow of insight to flood your consciousness.

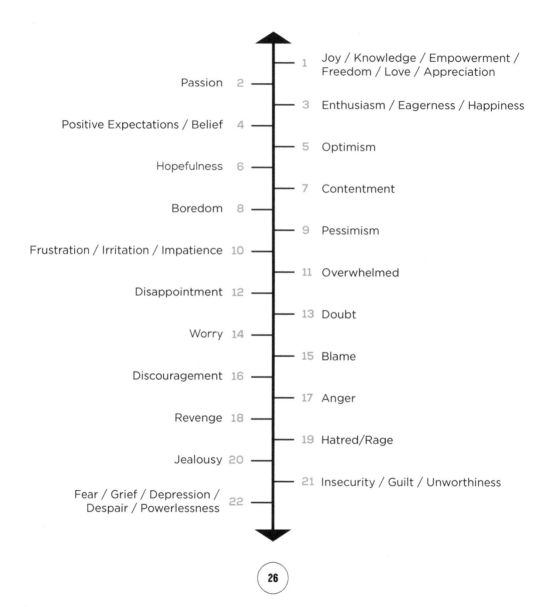

10
FEBRUARY

Emotional Tell

Emotions are a powerful part of who we are as humans. Throughout your mindfulness journey, you will learn to understand your emotions as tools to advise you of where you are in your vibration. See the "emotional scale" chart, adapted from the Abraham-Hicks Emotional Guidance Scale, pictured on page 26.

This scale explores all the emotions along steps of a ladder—with love and bliss at the top and depression and fear at the bottom. If you find yourself in a state of fear, you cannot expect to jump to bliss after one meditation or affirmation, but with consistent mindfulness practice, you will start to align with one higher-frequency emotion, followed by another, and so forth.

11
FEBRUARY

Today, turn to this affirmation for support: "I move beyond the illusion that I am alone and not a part of the universal whole. I know I am one with all. I am love. I choose love."

12

Flowing River

Find audio of river sounds to play during this meditation. Get comfortable in your seat with your feet on the floor and your hands in your lap. Close your eyes and allow any thoughts to drift away. Visualize a peaceful location with evergreen trees and explore the scenery in your mind. Notice a break in the trees that leads to a special river flowing with liquid love. This river will cleanse you of lower frequencies that no longer serve you. Enter the river and allow the cleansing water to effortlessly stream over you. Remain here for 10 minutes, and then tap into your Inner Knowing and ask yourself if the process is complete. *Feel* the answer. (See the resources on page 220.)

13
FEBRUARY

I have learned that the point of life's walk is not where or how far I move my feet but how I am moved in my heart.

—ANASAZI FOUNDATION,
THE SEVEN PATHS

14
FEBRUARY

~~~

Love Letter

The influence of words, when fueled by love, can be powerful. With mindful attention, write a love letter to yourself. Draw on experiences to access what you love about yourself and your life. This process is a precious gift, and no one is more worthy of receiving it!

15
FEBRUARY

~~~

Say not, "I have found the truth," but rather,
"I have found a truth."
Say not, "I have found the path of the soul." Say rather,
"I have met the soul walking upon my path."
For the soul walks upon all paths.
The soul walks not upon a line, neither does it
grow like a reed.
The soul unfolds itself, like a lotus of countless petals.

—KAHLIL GIBRAN, *THE PROPHET*

16
FEBRUARY

~~~

Strong Foundation

Yoga practices originated in ancient India. Just like a mindfulness practice that encompasses the mind, body, and spirit, there are yoga practices that explore the mental, physical, and spiritual aspects of our being. In today's exercise, I invite you to explore a simplified mountain pose, if you are comfortable doing so. This pose is the foundation of other standing poses. Here's how: Stand tall with your feet together. If you are having trouble balancing, stand with your feet slightly apart. Relax your shoulders and place your arms at your sides. Starting at your feet, evenly distribute your weight. Be consciously aware of your body stabilization as you work up from the feet. Take a deep breath and begin to slowly stretch your arms upward with your hands over your head, palms facing each other. Holding this pose, take an additional three deep breaths, then release. (See the resources on page 220 for more on mountain pose.)

17
FEBRUARY

~~~

Throughout the day, repeat this affirmation: "I am more than enough."

18
FEBRUARY

~~~

In your notebook, explore these questions: What are you willing to do to have peace in your life? Would you walk away from people who are negative, judgmental, and unsupportive? What if they are your family or your friends? Think through your answers. No one has the power to make you bitter, angry, or resentful. Only you have the power to allow those emotions to take hold and fester in you. Instead, seek love, forgiveness, and compassion. Your journey will unfold with graceful contentment, full of love for yourself and others who do not necessarily have to stay in your life.

19
FEBRUARY

~

He who cannot forgive breaks the bridge over which he himself must pass.

—GEORGE HERBERT

20
FEBRUARY

~

I Am a Priority

Make your mindfulness practice a priority by moving it to the top of your to-do list. Remind yourself to open this book and practice mindfulness every day. Schedule time in your calendar, set alarms and notifications, and slate "me" time. Give this time a special name if you want: "Meeting with Mindful Lee" or "Unfolding Appointment." Do it now, before you forget. And remember, you can practice mindfulness even without an appointment.

21
FEBRUARY

~~~

As you go about your day, repeat this affirmation silently: "I am open to receive love and kindness."

22
FEBRUARY

~~~

If you think you are too small to make a difference, try sleeping with a mosquito.

—DALAI LAMA XIV

23
FEBRUARY

~~~

Are you waiting for the storm to hit? Explore your patterns with respect to anticipating negative occurrences. Are you the person who says, "Call me when you get home so I know you are safe"? When you hear of an accident, do you immediately feel impending doom that your loved one is there? Explore this by journaling in your notebook. Are you always waiting for something negative to happen? Are you only looking at dark clouds or do you see breaks in them where the sun shines through? Consider that clouds eventually break apart and make way for the magic of the sun to reveal itself once again. Learn to honor the natural process through your mindfulness practice and self-observation; elevate your vibration and your resistant suffering will be no more. The contrast of life holds beauty and whispers secrets in the ebb of the experience. When we recognize the gift and stop pushing against it, the light reveals itself.

Inner and Outer World

The outer world reflects the inner-world experience. Draw a large gingerbread-man shape to represent you. Outside the gingerbread man, write single words or short phrases that represent the obstacles and challenges in your life. Inside the gingerbread man, write the feelings, self-limiting beliefs, and statements that could be the cause of your external reality. As you take time to explore yourself in this manner, gentle mindful awareness will pop in.

Throughout the day, repeat this affirmation: "An exciting chapter is unfolding in my life."

26
FEBRUARY

〜

Break free of old patterns by getting comfortable with change. Does any of the following sound familiar? You drive the same way to work or to your kid's school. You sit on the same couch cushion every night. You can do your gym routine in your sleep. You fill that glass of wine every day at the same time. The television is switched on without thought. Routine and rituals are helpful to enforce positive behaviors, but if they are limiting you by not allowing you to shift or engage change, or if the habit is not serving your highest good, it might be time to shake things up a bit. Grab your notebook and journal: Where might you want to release a limiting habit or pattern that is not serving you?

27
FEBRUARY

〜

Let yourself be silently drawn by the strange pull of what you really love. It will not lead you astray.

—RUMI

28
FEBRUARY

~~~

The Chains of Change

Change for the sake of change offers no wisdom. Embracing change as a by-product of your deliberate creation is part of your evolutionary process. As you journey through mindfulness practice, things will begin to shift because you are no longer a vibrational match for the old. If you resist change because you're too comfortable in old patterns, the change will not continue for your benefit. The progression will feel like one step forward and two back unless you embrace changes that bring you to your highest and best, which will propel you forward on your quest for inner peace and happiness. Today, experiment with change—for example, sit on a different side of the couch or wear a wristwatch instead of using your phone to tell the time. Let your thoughts gather on this topic. Explore areas in your life when you resisted a change that eventually became the optimal path for you. Which areas are you holding on to that are clearly not serving your highest good? (See the resources on page 221.)

MARCH

1
MARCH
~

Think about a time when you felt lucky. What was happening in your life when you were in that flow? Were you happy? Were you in love? Were you focused on your intentions? Louis Pasteur's quote "Chance favors the prepared mind" suggests that if you are focused and you put in the time to prepare, the outcome will be positive. Today, I invite you to expand that notion energetically. Your emotions, consciousness, and energy must be prepared to be in alignment for what you bring into your reality. In other words, if you desire a loving relationship that is honest, loyal, healthy, and communicative, you must prepare yourself to be in alignment with those very same qualities by being honest, loyal, healthy, and communicative.

2
MARCH
~

As you go about your day, repeat this affirmation silently: "I am abundant always and in all ways."

3
MARCH

~~~

Remember that sometimes not getting what you want is a wonderful stroke of luck.

—DALAI LAMA XIV

4
MARCH

~~~

Purify, Reprogram, and Affirm Prosperity

Find a glass drinking bottle you can write on or affix a label to. On the bottle or label, write the words Purify, Wellness, and Prosperity. Fill the bottle with filtered water. Let it sit for two hours before drinking. Drinking this water reinforces your intention to purify your energetic body, to reprogram old patterns that do not serve you, and to affirm prosperity. You can even add Lucky to the label if you'd like.

5
MARCH

~~~

State this affirmation aloud: "I honor exactly where I am at this moment as a part of my journey."

6
MARCH

~~~

Meditation is one of the simplest and most profound gifts you can honor yourself with, but it eludes many. In my experience, there are three main reasons people don't incorporate meditation into their daily lives: (1) they think that there is not enough time, (2) they feel that they cannot quiet the monkey-mind chatter, and (3) they believe they are not doing it right. What is your reason? All these self-imposed deterrents can be overcome with a consistent mindfulness practice. First, give yourself permission to be in practice. Then, release any attachment to outcome and the need to "conquer" or achieve meditation, which is the antithesis of meditation. It is in the surrender that you find peace. (See the resources on page 221 for more guidance.)

7
MARCH

~~~

Make this your mantra today: "Magical things happen for me every day."

8
MARCH

~~~

There is no way to prosperity, prosperity is the way.

—WAYNE DYER

MARCH

~~~

Chakra Awareness

In ancient Yogic tradition, chakra is a Sanskrit word that means spinning wheel of energy or light. In this spiritual wisdom, these seven main energy centers are a part of the human subtle body. Each chakra correlates with a color and is associated with particular emotions and body parts. For this exercise, this basic description is enough. If you have the time to delve deeper, study chakras. (See the resources on page 221.)

To begin, sit comfortably and close your eyes. Visualize a glowing area of colored light at each chakra location as the figure on page 44 shows. Breathe and visualize your breath going into one chakra at a time. Stay present and bring your awareness to any sensation you have. Allow at least one minute for each chakra.

MARCH

~~~

Today, turn to this affirmation for support: "All my needs and wants are met with ease and grace."

11
MARCH

~~~

What you resist, persists. Even if we desire to shift away from a negative person or habit, if we are consistently and constantly noodling about it, we're resisting it. Get your notebook and journal about what you are resisting. Where is your inner dialogue negatively taking you when you are facing a particular scenario? Do you find an inner conversation of judgment spewing about a situation or person? Are you reinforcing, with your thoughts and words, an outcome that you do not desire, such as "I am unlucky"? Just like the incessant fly that continues to buzz around your head as you swat the air, so shall the energy of your resistance fuel the very thing you wish to reject. Step back. Relax. Now, explore what changes you can make through mindfulness practice to shift this pattern in order to bring you to your desired outcome.

12
MARCH

~~~

Shallow men believe in luck . . . strong men believe in cause and effect.

—RALPH WALDO EMERSON

13
MARCH

~

Repeat to yourself throughout the day, "I move beyond the storm of chaos to the still waters of my soul."

14
MARCH

~

We must give to receive; we must nurture and respect ourselves, and others will honor us the same way. There is an ebb and flow to life. I invite you to look at ways you withhold your energy. Where are you feeling emptiness? Are you holding back and restricting your knowledge or creativity from flowing out into the world? Are you feeling lonely but not opening yourself to possibilities by declining invitations? Are you experiencing financial lack? Does it manifest as a resistant feeling in your body when you spend money? Do you withhold love because you have been hurt, and you fear the same will occur? Get your notebook and take some time to journal and explore.

15
MARCH

~

The trick is to make sure you don't die waiting for prosperity to come.

—LEE IACOCCA

16
MARCH

~

Play with the Inner World

Play a game today that I play all the time: Get quiet and connect with your Inner Self and ask, "What should I read today?" Check in with yourself until you feel an inner tug toward a book in your personal library, and feel the resonance in your body as you get closer to the chosen book. With mindful attention, you'll know which book is the one. It'll never fail to hold a perfect message in that moment. When I do this exercise, there are times I'll reach out to a book I've never read before or even knew I had. I may read a paragraph, a page, a chapter, or even the entire book. I always know when I have received the message. You will, too, with practice. If you don't have a personal library, you can do this exercise at a public library or in a bookstore.

17
MARCH

~~~

Make this your mantra today: "Just as a rainbow metaphorically ends at a pot of gold, so too shall my mindful journey reap glorious rewards."

18
MARCH

~~~

There is a quote I like by Master Saint Germain: "Life does not limit you! Opulence does not limit you! Love does not limit you! Therefore, why allow your human limiting concepts to bind you any longer?" Take a few moments to journal in your notebook about where you may be limiting yourself in your life experience.

19
MARCH

~~~

The Rose

This visualization exercise is in honor of my mother, Mille, whose birthday is on this day. Although she has transitioned from this life experience, her caring presence is always with me. My mother loved the stillness of the morning and so do I. There is a sense of renewal and peace that dwells in this time. If you are reading this after the morning hours, you can still visualize and find the essence of it in your mind.

Sit quietly, close your eyes, and take a few deep breaths to clear out any static. Now, begin to visualize a beautiful garden with a rosebush and the perfect bloom. Experience the beauty and scent of the rose with all your senses. For me, it would be the specimen that grew in my family yard when I was a young girl. My mother nurtured and cherished this one rosebush as if it were a prize—roses the color of coral, the petals like velvet, and the sweet scent beyond compare.

20
MARCH

~

I'm a greater believer in luck, and I find the harder I work
the more I have of it.

—THOMAS JEFFERSON

21
MARCH

~

Just let go. Let go of how you thought your life should be
and embrace the life that is trying to work its way into
your consciousness.

—CAROLINE MYSS

22
MARCH

~

In *Alice in Wonderland*, Lewis Carroll writes, "One day Alice came to a fork in the road and saw a Cheshire cat in a tree. "Which road do I take?" she asked. "Where do you want to go?" was his response. "I don't know," Alice answered. "Then," said the cat, "it doesn't matter." In your notebook, journal about what this passage means to you. Would you be okay with not knowing which path was better? Would it not matter? Guide your life with intention or ride the wave. Either way, it'll be an interesting journey.

23
MARCH

~

I am so proud of you and your progress and commitment to your daily mindfulness practice. Here's an affirmation to celebrate: "I am a magnificent mindful being, and I lead by example."

24
MARCH

~~~

Belly Laugh

When was the last time you had a good old-fashioned belly laugh? If you can't remember, it was most likely too long ago. Children and teenagers experience the freedom of a good laugh, but we, as adults, seem to have forgotten how to do this. It's believed that laughter has many health benefits, including boosting the immune system and reducing stress hormones. Simply put, laughter helps you feel better. Today, give it a go. Laugh. Laugh out loud! Notice how it is both blissfully cleansing and elevating. If you need help tickling your funny bone, watch a sitcom or cartoon you like. Find something that triggers a tear-provoking, belly-cramping laugh.

25
MARCH

~~~

If you worry that you are not good enough, I am here to tell you there is nothing you are not good enough for. State aloud: "I am deserving of all the wondrous things that flow to me with ease and grace."

26
MARCH

~~~

Take a step back from whatever is going on in your life. Breathe. Reflect. Look at all you have accomplished and how far you have come. The road ahead is always open to you, but if you are not frolicking on the path of life, you are missing out on the journey. Take some time to ponder this entry. In your notebook, jot down your thoughts and reactions to this message.

27
MARCH

~~~

We can control our lives by controlling our perceptions.

—BRUCE H. LIPTON

28
MARCH

~

Repeat to yourself throughout the day, "My journey *is* the destination."

29
MARCH

~

Are you placing your admiration, respect, and devotion on an individual or group and making them into an idol? Consider this carefully with mindful awareness. If this is the case for you, make an intention to seek out the beauty and wisdom that resonates in the message instead of the person. In your notebook, journal about ways in which you may have idealized a person or group instead of honoring the beauty and wisdom in the concepts and ideals they share.

30
MARCH

~~~

Prepare for Self-Care

Do you find yourself saying things like, "I just need to get through this and then I will take care of myself," or "I just need to get through this project/this event/this hurdle and then I will feel better"? This is an internal stress program. *Clamp down, stop breathing, push through* is the pattern of restriction. Stress is *not* a requirement to get the job done. Now more than ever is the time to stay mindful and practice self-love and self-care. Once you can prioritize mindfully taking care of yourself, the rest flows with more ease and grace. Today, make a list of at least five things you can do to care for yourself. Vary the activities from a few minutes to an hour, or longer if you wish. With this list, you'll be prepared ahead of time to access your self-care options. Make one self-care activity a priority today.

31
MARCH

~~~

I Am Open to Receive

Many of us may desire to bring something into our lives but do not feel worthy to receive it, thereby blocking the very thing we wish to bring into our reality. If you do this powerful exercise daily, it'll help clear that block. Try the exercise today and then incorporate it into your daily routine, such as in your morning shower!

Stand tall, shoulders back, chest out, heart open, head lifted slightly, arms by your side with palms out, and with your feet turned slightly outward, in alignment with your shoulders. State, "I am open to receive . . ." and fill in what you desire. Here are a few I use:

- I am open to receive and give love.
- I am open to receive optimal health and well-being.
- I am open to receive the optimal path to my highest expression.

Fill in the blank with what resonates with you. You'll notice that your day flows more easily. (See the resources on page 221 for my online program that includes this exercise.)

APRIL

1
APRIL

〜

All the world is made of faith, and trust, and pixie dust.

—J. M. BARRIE, *PETER PAN*

2
APRIL

〜

Here's a joke that has been told in many variations (I put my own spin on it, too): A troubled woman ventures out into nature to commune with the All-Knowing, every day pleading for financial relief: "Please, please, please . . . give me the grace to win the lottery." This lament goes on for months. Day after day, she begs and pleads. Finally, the All-Knowing shines light down upon the begging woman and says in an exasperated tone, "My dear, please, please, please . . . buy a ticket." We can trust and have faith in the process of life, but we must also do our part to bring our desires to fruition. Take a moment to reflect on where you are trusting that something will happen without your effort. In your note-book, jot down what you can do to support the desire with action.

3

APPRIL

~~~

Make this your mantra today: "I have the courage to lead a deliberate and resilient life with ease and grace."

4

APRIL

~~~

Resilience

Synonyms for resilience include strength, flexibility, toughness, and, interestingly, spirit. I believe we aren't taught how to flow through the rough times in life, and neither are we taught about the benefits of learning through the struggle. We are taught to seek ideals such as living "happily ever after." It's important to trust that the negative things that happen are purposeful and happen for us instead of to us. Stand tall, take a deep breath, and imagine yourself as a tall reed bending in the wind but never breaking. Then give yourself 15 minutes to reflect and journal in your notebook about the times when you were resilient. Once you have explored those times of resilience, cheer yourself on for the great job you are doing. Celebrate! Make yourself a cup of aromatic tea or take yourself to lunch and enjoy it with mindful attention.

5
APRIL

~~~

As you go about your day, repeat this affirmation silently: "I lead my life from a place of truth and authenticity."

6
APRIL

~~~

While we weather the winter months, we trust that spring will arrive again. We can ride out the less than optimal bumps along the road of life with the same understanding of renewal. Take time to journal and reflect on those challenging times from the past that seemed never ending. Did you spend time and energy on needless worry? How could that time have been better spent? How will you spend your time if you are faced with a similar situation in the future?

7
APRIL

~~~

It is time for parents to teach young people early on that in diversity there is beauty and there is strength. We all should know that diversity makes for a rich tapestry, and we must understand that all the threads of that tapestry are equal in value no matter their color.

—MAYA ANGELOU,
*WOULDN'T TAKE NOTHING
FOR MY JOURNEY NOW*

8
APRIL

~~~

Trust in Diversity

Trust that all things are working for the good of the whole. We need diversity in experiences and people. Today, hold this message in your consciousness. Where do you witness the importance of diversity? To really understand this concept, take a walk through a garden and explore the ecosystem. See how all its parts work together to support the whole.

9
APRIL

~

The best way to find out if you can trust somebody is to trust them.

—ERNEST HEMINGWAY

10
APRIL

~

In coaching my clients and in the early days of my personal mindfulness practice, I found a common pattern: the urge to rush through the process, whether it was emotional healing, personal development, or goal setting. The desire to get to the next level without fully experiencing the current stage was prevalent. If you do not trust the process of the unfolding, you are robbing yourself of the wisdom that the "now" holds. In your notebook, reflect on where you may be pushing through a process instead of savoring it. Then, set an intention to take the time to fully experience the journey.

11
APRIL

~~~

Repeat this affirmation to yourself throughout the day: "I trust the ebb, flow, and process of life."

12
APRIL

~~~

Exploring Trust

Sit comfortably, close your eyes, and breathe deeply for three breaths to relax your body. Adopt a mindful perspective—awareness without judgment. Ask yourself, "When in my life have I fully trusted the authenticity, character, and loyalty of another person and experienced a positive outcome?" Start with your childhood and move through each stage of your life. Now think of situations in which you were betrayed, a process that may evoke painful memories, so be gentle with yourself. In any of those situations, did you betray yourself by not listening to your Inner Knowing? Once you are finished with the review process, write down the lessons you learned from any significant memories. Look for patterns that connect each category of lesson. Remember, there's no judgment here, just awareness.

13
APRIL

~~~

Make this your mantra today: "I trust the freedom in being myself."

14
APRIL

~~~

Do you pretend to be someone you are not when you are with certain people? Are you wearing "masks" that reflect more of that person instead of who you truly are? Are you afraid that you are not likable as your authentic self? What parts of yourself are you holding back with certain people? Write down in your notebook whatever answers come to you, without judgment.

15

~

It can take courage and strength to move through betrayal, lies, infidel-ity, or mental illness in relationships. You might feel as though you can never trust again, but you still desire a loving, loyal relationship. Write the words *trust, faith*, and *hope*. Then, on a scale of 1 to 10, rate how you experience trust (1 means you don't experience trust at all). Now, try an experiment. As you navigate your day, notice when you are feeling trusting and when you are not, and make decisions in accordance with that feeling. Over time, your choices based on trust will form the person you wish to be and the person you wish to attract. Try this exercise with the words *faith* and *hope*, too.

16
APRIL

Trust You!

Have you been in situations where you can't make up your mind? Do you seek the guidance of friends and family over and over and value everyone else's opinion just a bit more than your own? You may feel that everyone—anyone—knows better than you. If this sounds familiar, begin to trust yourself. It may feel awkward, even scary, at first. Today, when a situation arises where you would typically seek advice from a friend, quiet yourself. Pause for a beat and do not react. Instead, spend some time in meditation. (See the resources on page 221 for suggestions.) Before beginning, state this intention: "I trust my guidance from my Inner Knowing and my own decisions that are for the highest and best of all concerned." As you meditate, release any attachment to the part of your mind that is thinking of that situation by paying attention to your breath. Relax. Just be. With this practice, you will find that clarity about the situation presents itself more easily.

17
APRIL

~~~

Repeat this affirmation throughout the day: "I trust that the Universe is always vying for my highest good."

18
APRIL

~~~

When we step into a doctor's office with a health complaint, we trust that whatever ails us will be resolved. That trust begins the healing. Today, I invite you to ponder what it means to trust yourself. Through your faith in the process of mindfulness, you will bring forth the relief you are seeking—whether it is physical, emotional, mental, or spiritual. You will be guided (just as you were to this book) to the answers you need and can act upon.

19
APRIL

~~~

Parking Angel

A parking angel is often credited for providing a driver with an amazing parking place. Today, I invite you to release any restrictive limits and judgments and play this game. Trust in the power of the mind's intention. Trust that you will find a perfect parking space today that you usually never access at work, in a crowded grocery store lot, or during a weekend at the local superstore. Don't be surprised if there is an SUV exiting just as you come up the row!

20
APRIL

~~~

Love cannot live where there is no trust.

—EDITH HAMILTON, *MYTHOLOGY*

21
APRIL

In mindfulness practice, we bring nonjudgmental awareness to the moment. Today, I invite you to mindfully explore your emotions in this manner. You are far more than what you see with the limited five senses. One of the beginning ways to connect to the deeper levels of ourselves is by understanding our emotions. So in your notebook, write the following three questions on a fresh page and explore your relationship with them through journaling.

- "Do I value my emotions? How do I do this?"
- "Do I dismiss my emotions, block them, or push them away?"
- "Are my emotions signaling an area to explore more deeply?"

22
APRIL

Make this your mantra today: "I trust my authentic self will guide me to my tribe."

23
APRIL

~~~

Trust yourself, you will start to trust others.

—SANTOSH KALWAR

24
APRIL

~~~

Discernment

Are you feeling mistrustful in any way? If so, here is a brief exercise to support you: Close your eyes. Visualize the words *faith*, *hope*, *trust*, and *loyalty* above your head as different-colored sparkling lights that are showering their light upon you. Let your imagination choose the color for each word, one after another or all at once. Do this for a minute and feel the mistrust dissolving. Now visualize the word *discernment*. See it as a bright white light showering upon you. In this case, discernment is not judgment; it is awareness of alignment. It's the ability to have the Inner Knowing of whether a situation or person is in the highest and best alignment for you. As you strengthen your mindfulness practice, you'll get better at understanding this subtle difference.

25
APRIL

~~~

As you go about your day, repeat this affirmation silently:
"I surround myself with trusting, loyal, and mindful people."

26
APRIL

~~~

To have faith is to trust yourself to the water. When you
swim, you don't grab hold of the water, because if you do,
you will sink and drown. Instead you relax, and float.

—ALAN WILSON WATTS

27
APRIL

~~~

The inability to open up to hope is what blocks trust, and blocked trust is the reason for blighted dreams.

—ELIZABETH GILBERT

28
APRIL

~~~

Today, turn to this affirmation for support: "I forgive and release all blocks related to betrayal and disloyalty from myself and others."

29
APRIL

~~~

Wait

Today, practice allowing yourself the time it takes for you to gain clarity about a situation or a decision. Though we may often want to act on something quickly, sometimes it is best to not react right away and simply wait. Begin to notice when you want to immediately react to a person or situation. Instead of reacting, breathe with awareness for a few moments to let your Inner Knowing catch up with the situation. Know that the best response, information needed, or resolution will present itself at the optimal time. Trust that awareness and clarity will emerge.

30
APRIL

~~~

You can only trust your emotions as you can lie to yourself with your brain but not your heart.

—CARL WHITE

MAY

1
MAY

Make this your mantra today: "I have confidence in my Inner Knowing to direct me on my optimal path."

2
MAY

Great discoveries were brought forth with the craziness of making known the unknown. It is progress. In your notebook, journal about where you have stifled your intuition, your Inner Knowing, about something that turned out to be the correct direction for you. Explore great inventors, scientists, and thinkers who were once thought of as crazy for their hypotheses, but who are now known as visionary geniuses in their field—for example, Gregor Mendel, Albert Einstein, Nikola Tesla, and Elon Musk.

3

MAY

~~~

I tell you, in this world, being a little crazy helps to keep you sane.

—ZSA ZSA GABOR

4

MAY

~~~

Dear Me

Write a letter to your Inner Knowing. It might read something like this:

Dear Inner Knowing,

My sincere apologies for taking so long to communicate. You have been quite patient with me. It was not purposeful; I just forgot you were there. Thank you for silently nudging me in the best direction through my gut feelings, intuitive senses, and synchronicities. I now know it was you trying to get my attention. I will now do my part—silence my mind, so I can connect more fully.

With my love and gratitude,
Me

5
MAY

〜〜〜

Repeat this affirmation throughout the day: "I am in the process of mindfully unfolding."

6
MAY

〜〜〜

Have you ever experienced a great idea that came out of nowhere? Was it really from nowhere? Our Inner Knowing is connected to all wisdom, but we often think that our intellect and our mind is the limit of our knowledge capacity. When you release that perceived restriction by opening your perspective, you will tap into the wisdom of universal expanse. Like anything else, this release requires practice to gain proficiency. If there is constant external noise and distraction, you will not have the silence needed to hear the wisdom. So, take a moment to quiet yourself. Begin by connecting to your breath. Now ask your Inner Knowing for an inspired thought today. Then let go of any control or attachment to outcome or time limits. Just ask and let it go. See what happens. Keep your notebook nearby throughout the day to jot down anything that comes to you.

7
MAY

Change your thoughts and you change your world.

—NORMAN VINCENT PEALE

8
MAY

Wisdom Writing

For this exercise, start with a meditation to clear the clutter from your mind and be open to the flow of inspired thought and wisdom from your Inner Knowing. (See the resources on page 221.) After your meditation, write down a question in your notebook whose answer has previously eluded you. Then close your eyes, take a deep breath, and listen. Wait until you are inspired to write an answer. Don't grasp or reach for an answer. Surrender in peace. Continue this exercise for at least 15 minutes until you make the connection, or step away and try again later. You can do this exercise for 45 minutes to an hour. Consistent practice is more important than the length of time you practice this exercise.

9
MAY

Make this your mantra today: "I am creating my highest expression of self with ease and grace."

10
MAY

The purpose of one's life can be elusive. Many people get caught up in a chosen career based purely on obligation. They spend their lives following someone else's idea of their life purpose, but an urging deep within them craves a more fulfilling path. Having clarity around your life's purpose removes that feeling of dread that can occur when it's time to go to work. When you are on your path of life's purpose, your work becomes a fluid dance that is empowering, joyful, and fulfilling. Understanding your purpose could result in a change of job or perhaps merely a perspective. Explore this idea while journaling today. Are you on your optimal path?

11
MAY

~~~

Life is too important to be taken seriously.

—OSCAR WILDE

12
MAY

~~~

Follow Your Gut

Have you ever walked into a room or met someone new and were suddenly connected in a way that felt joyful, authentic, and familiar? Maybe the opposite has occurred: You met someone and instantly had a visceral feeling of iciness. Maybe you felt a negative vibe immediately but had no idea why. This is your intuition, your Inner Knowing. It is meant to guide and signal you. Have you ever ignored the negative feelings and forged ahead, and then wondered why there wasn't a positive outcome? Today, honor your gut feelings. Be aware of when you are connected intuitively, and act based on your Inner Knowing. Don't act out of fear from the mind, but rather acknowledge that this sense is guiding you.

13
MAY
~~~

It's time to stretch the mind and spirit. Extend your perspective and broaden the scope of what is possible by asking yourself some "what if" questions. Have fun with this exercise! Be mindfully aware of nonjudgment and allow yourself to explore ideas. What if you were a superhero? What if there were no wars, hatred, disease, or famine in the world? What if you could do and be anything you wanted? Ask yourself these questions and journal your answers. Take it a step further and allow other ideas that stretch your beliefs to bubble up in your consciousness.

14
MAY
~~~

Repeat this affirmation throughout the day: "I forgive myself and others as I am aware that holding grudges limits my growth and happiness."

15
MAY

~~~

Essential Oils

Explore the powerful benefits of essential oils for your mind, body, and spirit. It is imperative that you do your homework so you can use essential oils responsibly, both for your health and that of your pets. I suggest you choose high-quality essential oils that are organic, pure, and not mixed with carrier oils, whenever available. I have used Young Living Essential Oils for many years and turn to the *Essential Oils Desk Reference* and the *Essential Oils Integrative Medical Guide* as my reference books (see the resources on page 222). This evening, start by diffusing lavender essential oil an hour before you go to bed. You can usually find lavender essential oil in supermarkets that offer earth-friendly foods and products. Don't have a diffuser? Put a few drops on a paper towel and leave it under your pillow. Sweet dreams.

16
MAY

~~~

State and affirm this phrase: "I honor and respect myself through my daily meditation practice and make it a priority in my life."

17
MAY

~

Connecting with your Inner Knowing through a mindfulness practice can lead to heightened intuition and psychic awareness. In your notebook, explore your beliefs around intuition and psychic ability. Do you feel they are negative? Do you feel they are a gift? If you were more intuitive or psychic, how would your life improve?

18
MAY

~

Intentional Meditation

Regardless of how much you want it, change will occur only when you implement the necessary tools in your daily practice. Today, do your meditation while listening to music without guidance. (See the resources on page 222 for suggestions.) Prior to beginning, state three times: "I take full responsibility for my health and well-being—mind, body, and spirit. I release all attachments to victim mentality and the blame of others. I embrace all experiences that led me to the lessons I have learned and to this point of awakening to who I truly am. I value all life as I value my own." Allow these words to wash over you as you surrender to the music.

19
MAY

~~~

Be happy for this moment. This moment is your life.

—OMAR KHAYYAM

20
MAY

~~~

Stretch Your Body

It is important to stretch the body, mind, and spirit. Today, let's address the body with some gentle movement. (See the resources on page 222 for some guidance on stretching, and consult your chiropractor or physician to determine the most appropriate exercises and stretches for you.)

Before you begin, do a short aerobic warm-up such as jogging in place, jumping rope, or taking a brisk walk. After your warm-up, sit with your legs straight out in front of you. Starting with your toes, move rhythmically from body part to body part, gently stretching each part. Take a deep breath with each purposeful progression. Move to your ankles, legs, back, arms, fingers, and up to your neck. As you do, listen to your body; where is it tight? Give that area additional love and attention. Afterward, acknowledge your body for the magnificent job it is doing.

21
MAY

〜

Know when to walk away, know when to take another path, and know when you have learned the lesson that you were meant to learn. When you truly understand eternity of the soul, experience becomes the goal. Wisdom and knowledge become the outcome. In your notebook, journal about what these statements mean to you.

22
MAY

〜

Have you put yourself second, or last for that matter? Look at your patterns of behavior pertaining to self-respect and self-love. If these patterns are not optimal, explore why this is the case. Keep in mind that lack of self-worth can disguise itself with a mask of overconfidence or control through perfectionism. In your notebook, write down the times you haven't prioritized yourself. When did the lack of self-love and self-worth rear its head for the first time? How has that pattern continued throughout your life? Are you ready to shift that pattern?

23
MAY

Life can only be understood backwards; but it must be lived forwards.

—SØREN KIERKEGAARD

24
MAY

Your Body Knows

Your body may be voicing discomfort. Because the link between your emotions and your body is strong, addressing your emotional issues will help heal your physical ailments. That lower back pain may be telling you to address fear about money. The chronic migraine could be your body reacting to control issues. A sinus problem may be caused by irritation toward a person close to you.

To explore physical manifestations of emotional issues and to find healing affirmations, I recommend Louise Hay's *You Can Heal Your Life*. Use the affirmations in conjunction with, not as a substitute for, necessary medical care.

25
MAY

Repeat this affirmation throughout the day: "I am limitless. I create my reality with my thoughts and words."

26
MAY

One of my favorite movies is *What Dreams May Come* starring Robin Williams. When I saw the movie for the first time, I cried intensely and had an overwhelming feeling of "knowing" that this movie held truth. Ten years later, my near-death experience occurred, and I understood. There is no death. Only life. If this is your belief, how did you come to this awareness? What steps led you to the knowledge? If you do not reso-nate with this belief, in mindful, nonjudgmental awareness, journal in your notebook what it would mean to you if this belief was the truth.

27
MAY
~~~

It always seems impossible until it's done.

—NELSON MANDELA

28
MAY
~~~

Make this your mantra today: "I am pure potentiality. There are no limits to what I am or what I can create when I do so from a source of love and service."

29
MAY

~~~

Are you in bondage by the chains of victim mentality? Are you placing blame infused with anger, sadness, and resentment toward external forces, situations, and people for all failures? Once you find freedom from this cycle, your healing begins. Get your notebook and begin to reflect through journaling. When you acknowledge the common denominator of the stories you tell yourself, you'll realize all the stories have a shared thread. Unhappy with your current situation? Change the pattern. Change the life. Period.

30
MAY

~~~

Difficult and meaningful will always bring more satisfaction than easy and meaningless.

—MAXIME LAGACÉ

31
MAY

~

Distraction, disruption, and interference—these are all ways we self-sabotage and stifle our growth, personal development, and spiritual awakening. Our internal program that says we have limits keeps us small and unable to reach our goals. Like the dog in the movie *Up*, who constantly loses his focus when he sees a squirrel, daily distractions hold us back from strengthening our mindful foundation. Stay the course and keep practicing. What are some of your distractions? In your notebook, jot down these distractions. Then write the following and state it aloud: "I am motivated and dedicated to my mindfulness practice and make it a priority in my life. I clearly see the distractions that do not serve my goals, and I easily come back to focus."

JUNE

1
JUNE

Up to the Stars

Prepare for meditation by stating: "For as many stars as there are in the infinite Universe, so shall there be awakened souls and Light for all human-kind." Set a timer for 10 to 20 minutes. Play gentle instrumental music. (See the resources on page 222 for a suggestion.)

Sit comfortably with your feet on the ground and hands in your lap. Close your eyes and take three deep breaths. Allow thoughts to move by without consideration, and bring your awareness back to the *now*. Next, envision the night sky and allow your consciousness to drift up to the stars. Acknowledge their beauty. Repeat, "Light for all humankind," as often as you desire before journeying back to your body. Take a deep breath. Stretch and gently open your eyes when you are ready.

2
JUNE

The Light in you is the unalterable truth of who you are. You can deny it and obscure it, but you cannot uncreate it.

—MARIANNE WILLIAMSON

3

JUNE

Sanctuary

If you haven't already done so, create a space in your home that is espe-
cially for you. The space could be a corner of a room or the entire room.
It is yours. You decide. If you notice resistance, avoid judging yourself or
your space. Acknowledge the resistance and allow it to pass. When you
set up your space with mindful attention, you will create a sanctuary that
feels peaceful, loving, and light—a place where you meditate, journal, and
commune with your Inner Knowing. Think of this as your happy place until
you don't need it anymore, because you've found the sanctuary within.
With every purposeful step along your path, create your sanctuary as an
opportunity to strengthen your mindfulness practice. There's no need to
rush. Be deliberate in your creation, but start today.

4

JUNE

**Raise your words, not your voice. It is rain that grows
flowers, not thunder.**

—RUMI

5
JUNE

~~~

Contemplate the following edited excerpt from my book The Temple of All Knowing. Then journal what it means to you.

Love enters us from a well of existence that is streaming from the natural Source. We do not own it; it flows freely and is given with no requirement or judgment of its use. It is the life force of all creation. This life force runs through every living being in the cosmos. If you could glimpse for just one moment, the purity of the Light of all existence—it would most definitely change you. The worry and the fear that penetrates every layer of your current existence would vanish like a streak of lightning in the night sky. It would melt all the worry and darkness from your heart and fill you with the Light of love for all mankind . . . Your limited knowing of what the Light is, is the only problem or issue that you need to resolve. The only issue.

6
JUNE

~~~

Dimming your Inner Light is a tragedy for humanity. Make this your mantra today: "I shine my light brightly for all to experience."

7
JUNE

〜

In 2008, I had a near-death experience, and in the experience, my spirit left my body. I was Light, encased in Light and Light was all around. There were variations of Light all around. I felt freedom and experienced nonattachment. Today, I encourage you to ponder the word *Light* and what it means to you. Think beyond a lightbulb and the light brought forth from the night into the day. Write down all the meanings you have for *Light*. There are no wrong answers.

8
JUNE

〜

Contemplating Death

What if there was no death? I believe that knowing there is no death is an element of spiritual awakening. That's why I use the terms *passed on, transitioned,* or *in nonphysical form* to describe those who have "died." In this exercise, write a letter to a loved one who has passed on. Ask them to provide a sign as a recognition of their connection, such as a number or an animal to show they are near. For example, I know my mother is close when I encounter mourning doves.

9
JUNE

~

If men only felt about death as they do about sleep, all
terrors would cease . . . Men sleep contentedly, assured
that they will wake the following morning. They should
feel the same about their lives.

—RICHARD MATHESON,
WHAT DREAMS MAY COME

10
JUNE

~

Repeat these powerful statements throughout the day: "I am Love
in Motion. I am Illuminated!"

11
JUNE

~

Within you is the light of the world—the only light that can be shed upon the Path. If you are unable to perceive it within you, it is useless to look for it elsewhere.

—MABEL COLLINS,
*LIGHT ON THE PATH AND
THROUGH THE GATES OF GOLD*

12
JUNE

~

In your notebook, jot down something that is disrupting your peace. Below that, write, "So what?!" Will you remember this disruption in a week, a month, a year? Ease up on yourself and have a little fun with life. Be honest: Are you making a mountain out of a molehill? Have you blown a minor inconvenience or grievance out of proportion? If so, remember, life is not all that serious. Change your perspective on the situation and have a laugh.

13
JUNE

~~~

Release

Just as you wash your physical body, it is extremely important to cleanse your energetic body every day. We are constantly bombarded with negative energies. When we pick up these energies, they can impact our mood. One minute you are feeling great, and the next, you run into an acquaintance at the grocery store who unloads some emotional baggage on you, and you are left carrying some of that baggage home. Although there are various ways to cleanse yourself, such as healing meditations, smudging, or Reiki energy clearing, you can do a quick clearing today.

Set this intention: "I clear all energies that do not serve me through the Universal Light." Now, envision a brilliant white light dropping down from far above you. Allow it to enter your body from the top of your head. Envision another light coming up from the earth and entering your body from your feet. Visualize this light permeating all aspects of yourself. Say, "Release, release, release." The light, at this higher vibration, will fill the void of any removed energies.

14
JUNE

~~

Repeat this affirmation throughout the day: "I am creating my ultimate life with ease and grace."

15
JUNE

~~

Reflect on this insight of Nathaniel Hawthorne: "Happiness is a butterfly, which when pursued, is always just beyond your grasp, but which, if you will sit down quietly, may alight upon you." Take a few moments in stillness. What is it that you are grasping for? Happiness in general? Is it something that you have been wanting and asking for that has eluded you thus far? Doodle a butterfly in your notebook, copy down the quote, and reflect upon the greatness of life. Then write, "Happiness resides within me."

16
JUNE

~

Namaste

This Hindu greeting used in words and gestures means "I bow to you."
The significance and definition have expanded to "I acknowledge and
honor the Divine spark in you." Today, practice this gesture in the mirror
by placing your hands together in front of the center of your brow. Close
your eyes and move your hands to your heart area while bowing your
head slightly. Say, "Namaste" to your reflection. Even though this yoga
tradition is not a requirement of a mindfulness practice, it is a beautiful
gesture to acknowledge your own Divine spark.

17
JUNE

~

Today, turn to this affirmation for support: "I move toward what
lights me up. I move away from what dims my Light."

18
JUNE

~~~

Don't Despair, Help Is Here

When you find yourself feeling low, emotionally challenged, or in a dark storm, try not to despair. The rainbow will come, and the sun will rise again. When I was at the lowest point of my life, it was hard to imagine that things would get better. I followed the bread crumbs of a slightly better feeling and never let go of the vision of my dreams. I focused on my daily mindfulness practice, self-love, and self-care, and I felt guided to consciousness raising and emotional healing. I surrendered to the journey without judgment as best as I could, and the Light revealed itself once again. If you are feeling low, here are three things you can do immediately to help:

- Meditate (see the resources on page 222 for suggestions).
- In your notebook, list three things you are grateful for today.
- Take a walk in nature.

19
JUNE

~~~

The teacher who is indeed wise does not bid you to enter the House of his wisdom but rather leads you to the threshold of your mind.

—KHALIL GIBRAN

20
JUNE

~~~

Every individual's journey is different. There is not just one path to expanding your consciousness or ultimate enlightenment. What is offered in this book is a collection of the wisdom I gleaned from education and exploration along my path while successfully supporting others. It is most important to connect with your Inner Knowing and to recognize what resonates. What doesn't resonate may be a seed for later growth. Honor your own guidance; it is powerful. Take a moment to journal what this statement means to you: "I am a sovereign independent being and take full responsibility for my life path to higher consciousness." If the statement resonates with you, write it down in your notebook and explore the depth of its meaning.

21
JUNE

~~~

Read, recite, and repeat this affirmation: "I am a unique emanation of Light. I am perfect in all ways and always. As I self-observe, mindfully develop, and spiritually expand, I understand and embrace the truth of who I am."

22
JUNE

There is no question but these people have brought the Light through the long ages, and they prove by their daily life and works that this Light does exist just as it did thousands of years ago.

—BAIRD T. SPALDING, *LIFE AND TEACHING OF THE MASTERS OF THE FAR EAST*

23
JUNE

〜〜〜

As you go about your day, repeat this affirmation silently: "In the disparity of my life, I see the wisdom and knowledge of each experience."

24
JUNE

〜〜〜

Observe

As you go about your day today, be the Observer. To do this, consciously take a step back, and instead of instantly reacting to a stimulus and participating in every conversation or exchange, simply observe those around you. Monitor yourself in the experience. Be mindfully aware of others and yourself without judgment. Speak less and listen more. With a consistent mindfulness practice, being the Observer will become a more natural part of your interactions.

25
JUNE

~~~

What's your favorite color? Each color has a frequency. The color violet has the highest frequency of visible light on the spectrum of color. Violet is also associated with the crown chakra. The crown chakra is the seventh of the seven major chakras and is associated with connection to the Divine. Which color do you most resonate with? When you meditate, do you see colors? Which ones? Explore these questions in your notebook. If you want to take this further, you can explore light frequency and chakras.

26
JUNE

~~~

Make this your mantra today: "I am an eternal being of Light. I am one with the Light of all Consciousness."

27
JUNE

~~~

The act of self observation is the only change a human being needs to make in her behavior; everything else, all fundamental changes in behavior, emotion, and thinking arise as a by-product of this practice. In other words, self observation is radical, revolutionary, evolutionary, and fundamental change in the inner world of the human biological instrument.

—RED HAWK, *SELF OBSERVATION*

28
JUNE

~~~

To allow your pathway to present itself, repeat this affirmation: "I am guided to the appropriate pathway to balance and clear my energy centers through synchronicity and Inner Knowing. And so it is."

29
JUNE

~~~

I would not consider myself an artistic person, but I have been lucky enough to attract exquisite visual artists and conscious spiritual beings who express their talents in extraordinary ways. I love to explore the use of color and shading in their creations. Studying nature is another way to honor color. How do you explore color in your life? Has it become mundane? What if you became color blind and only saw in shades of gray? Today, heighten your appreciation of color.

30
JUNE

~~~

Through all the darkness, through all the shame of which men are capable, the spirit of man will remain alive on this earth. It may sleep, but it will awaken. It may wear chains, but it will break through.

—AYN RAND

JULY

1
JULY

~

Those who do not move, do not notice their chains.

—ROSA LUXEMBURG

2
JULY

~

Look at where you are bound by your viewpoint. Take a few moments to reflect and journal in your notebook using the following question as a catalyst: Are you locked in, stifled, and confined by an old belief or someone's imposed conviction?

3
JULY

~~~

Repeat this affirmation throughout the day: "I am free to explore other viewpoints through the mindfulness lens of nonjudgment."

4
JULY

~~~

Through journaling in your notebook, explore your feelings about the word independence and how you've defined it in your mind. Often the definition of words and the cultural translations are skewed over the years. People embrace the meaning of words without deliberate conscious understanding. Spend a few minutes researching the definition of independence. After reading it, close your eyes, take a deep breath, release any resistance, and stay in mindful nonjudgment. Visualize what independence means to you. Ask yourself, "Is this what I believe to be true?" Release any attachment to what you have been taught or believed about the word. Does the word still resonate in the same manner?

5

~~~

Mindful Eating

Do you rush through meals or appease your "hangry monster" with fast food or other less-than-optimal choices? Do you then feel guilty? Do you consume countless calories while mindlessly binge-watching a television series? Today, start to become deliberate with your eating and honor the process of fueling your sacred body. Listen to your body and do not resist hunger when it arises. Acknowledge your hunger by providing it with a healthy meal. If you can, have your meal alone during this initial exercise so that you are not distracted. Slow down, sit down, and chew with intention. Feel appreciative for this food—for all the people and possibly animals and plants it took to provide the food. Give thanks for every aspect of the meal. Throughout the rest of the day, listen to your body and cravings with respect to your food and drink consumption. For instance, do you crave sugar, carbs, or caffeine? How long have you been reacting to this craving? Does it have a hold on you, or do you have control of it?

6
JULY

Today, turn to this affirmation for support: "I need not blindly follow the path of others to feel loved and included. I release myself from this limited thinking and allow my inner guidance to liberate me."

7
JULY

To experience conscious liberation, one must feel comfortable in one's own skin. If you are not already in this space of acceptance, the unfolding of it is a process. Explore all aspects of yourself—mind, body, and spirit. Think through the perceived good, bad, and ugly. Mindful awareness, or self-observation, in nonjudgment is a tool you can use to assist in this process. In your notebook, explore the following questions as they pertain to your comfort with your individuality. In what areas of your life are you afraid to step forward and express yourself in your truth? Have you become a follower to the extent that you're no longer aware of your own perceptions, tastes, and likes?

8
JULY

~

Laugh at yourself and at life. Not in the spirit of derision or whining self-pity, but as a remedy, a miracle drug, that will ease your pain, cure your depression, and help you to put in perspective that seemingly terrible defeat and worry with laughter at your predicaments, thus freeing your mind to think clearly toward the solution that is certain to come.

—OG MANDINO

9
JULY

~

Laughter, the Great Liberator

There is so much emotional freedom felt in an erupting belly laugh. For this exercise, set an intention to add playful humor to your day. Everyone has a different sense of humor, so find what works for you. When I want a belly laugh, I "ask" the Universe to provide it for me. Sometimes, I am the instrument for a good laugh. I have a friend who places plastic googly eyes on unassuming targets such as a coffee mug, refrigerator, or water dispenser.

10
JULY

~~~

The cause of bandha and moksha (bondage and liberation) is our own minds. If we think we are bound, we are bound. If we think we are liberated, we are liberated. . . . It is only when we transcend the mind that we are free from all these troubles.

—SRI SWAMI SATCHIDANANDA,
THE YOGA SUTRAS OF PATANJALI

11
JULY

~~~

You may have heard the phrase "There is good in everyone." I would also add that there is bad in everyone—what Carl Jung calls the shadow self. View this self as a fountain of wisdom. What if the road to liberation, enlightenment, and happiness is in the exploration and acceptance of the shadow self? What if suffering comes from the judging? Take out your notebook and, as you journal, observe the parts of you you've been hiding from the world and yourself. (See the resources on page 222 for further reading on the shadow shelf.)

12
JULY

~~~

Make this affirmation part of your daily practice. The further along you are on your mindfulness-based path, the more profound this mantra will be: "Life is but experience. The purpose is in the exploration. The gift is in the contrast."

13
JULY

~~~

Journey on a Cloud

Attention to the stress, worry, and suffering in life is what makes the stress, worry, and suffering real. To change the outcome, shift your perspective. Set aside 10 minutes today to experience my guided meditation "Journey on a Cloud" (See the resources on page 222 for the link.) This meditation will help you develop a deeper understanding of how to lift stress, worry, and other forms of suffering. Prepare for meditation as usual by sitting comfortably in your seat with your feet on the ground and your hands on your lap, with your spine and neck straight. Press play and begin your journey.

14
JULY

Take a few moments to journal and explore your feelings and awareness that arise with this consciousness-expanding prompt: What if everything you were taught in history books, mathematics, science, and the nature of reality was false? Ponder what you have been raised to believe about the purpose of life, optimal health, and our capabilities as humans. What if it was an elaborate misdirection? Would you feel betrayed? Or could you tap into the explorer in you and feel exhilarated by the possibility of shattering an illusion?

15
JULY

Let us not seek to satisfy our thirst for freedom by drinking from the cup of bitterness and hatred.

—MARTIN LUTHER KING JR.

16
JULY

~~~

Bliss: A State of Mind

Have you ever heard a piece of music that completely shifted your state of mind? Do you have a song that takes you back to an experience or a time that elevated your mood and you felt pure happiness? In this exercise, listen to a favorite bliss-invoking song. Pay attention to the tones, sound, rhythm, and lyrics. Is it the resonance of the musical composition or the meaning of the words that connects you? Enjoy every second of it.

17
JULY

Repeat this affirmation throughout the day: "I am using good judgment to decide with whom I spend my precious time."

18
JULY

~~~

Turn Off the Tap

Has someone depleted your energy? If your Inner Light is dim and you feel listless and powerless in the company of another, somewhere within you, you gave that person permission to drain you. It can happen subtly when you are not mindful of where you are expending your energy. If this depletion has been going on for a while, you may not even recognize yourself because your Inner Light has diminished. However, you are a spiritual warrior, stronger than you can imagine. If this question resonates with you, you can close and release the energetic siphon with your intention. State aloud in the sanctity of your own space: "I no longer give you permission to draw upon my energy. I am a sacred, liberated being of Light."

19
JULY

~~~

If you have never fallen and risen, time and time again, you've never learned to walk.

—JERRY METELLUS

20
JULY

~~~

As you go about your day, repeat this affirmation silently: "I lead by example through my mindfulness practice and explorative journey of self."

21
JULY

~~~

Where are you attached to your story? In your notebook, journal on a current negative situation. Has someone not returned your phone call or e-mail? Have you felt ghosted by a friend? Are you waiting for signatures on a contract? Did you expect a compliment and not receive it? What story are you telling yourself about the situation? Where are you filling in the gaps of the unknown circumstances? Is it real or is it just a story you are telling yourself?

22
JULY

~

Mindful Food Prep

Have you ever heard someone claim that they put love into the dishes they make, and that's why their food tastes so good? Today, prepare a meal with mindfulness. Feel love and joy in every aspect of the preparation as you move slowly around the kitchen. Allow your heart to fill with gratitude that you have the essentials needed to create this meal. Even if you are preparing a simple broth, adding love and appreciation with mindful awareness will energetically supplement the broth and nourish all who consume it.

23
JULY

~

The real liberation dwells in the discipline.

—NEERAJ AGNIHOTRI, *PROCRASDEMON:*
THE ARTIST'S GUIDE TO LIBERATION
FROM PROCRASTINATION

24
JULY

Break through the limits of the mind, step into your independence day, and the ultimate light show will be yours. In your notebook, journal about what it means to you to be free of limiting thoughts and how your life would look if you were completely independent. How will your light show display itself?

25
JULY

Make this your mantra today: "I transcend the illusion of the current experience that does not serve my greatest good."

26

JULY

~~~

Walking Meditation

Today, find a designated and defined area where you will not be disturbed by pedestrians, and create a path specifically for a mindfulness-based walking meditation. This is not like a walk for exercise but rather a walk to focus your attention on your movements. Pay close attention to the movements of your feet, legs, and arms. Walk at a slow and methodical pace for 10 minutes. You might integrate a walking meditation into your mindfulness practice by doing it once a week or once a month, gradually working up to 30 minutes. Walking meditation is a complementary practice for seated meditation; it does not replace it.

27

JULY

~~~

Rethink perfection. Understand that each is a part of the whole, and repeat this affirmation to yourself: "I embrace the uniqueness of who I am. I honor the diversity of all beings."

28
JULY

~~~

For you can only be free when even the desire of seeking freedom becomes a harness to you, and when you cease to speak of freedom as a goal and a fulfillment. You shall be free indeed when your days are not without a care nor your nights without a want and a grief, but rather when these things girdle your life and yet you rise above them naked and unbound.

—KAHLIL GIBRAN,
THE PROPHET

29
JULY

~~~

Journal in your notebook and explore your thoughts on what you feel the philosopher Kahlil Gibran was conveying in yesterday's quote in which he poetically describes freedom. (See the resources on page 222 for a link to the full text.) Does this message resonate with you?

30
JULY

~~~

Liberate yourself as far as you can, and you have done your part; for it is not given to every one to break through all limits, or, more expressively, not to every one is that a limit which is a limit for the rest. Consequently, do not tire yourself with toiling at the limits of others. . . . He who overturns one of his limits may have shown others the way and the means; the overturning of their limits remains their affair.

—MAX STIRNER,
THE EGO AND ITS OWN

31
JULY

~~~

Breath of Life

While sitting, expand your chest and belly with breaths for at least five minutes. With each inhale, give thanks, and with each exhale, release apathy. The breath holds whispers of peace in the silence.

AUGUST

1
AUGUST

〜

Your vision will become clear only when you can look into your own heart. Who looks outside, dreams; who looks inside, awakes.

—CARL JUNG

2
AUGUST

〜

Philosophers, spiritual gurus, and now quantum theorists have said that this life is only an illusion—a dream, if you will, made from the mind. If this is fact, how would you change the way you experience your life? Would the knowledge that the mind is creating your reality make you more cautious and deliberate with your thoughts? Journal in your note-book about these questions.

3
AUGUST

~~~

Dreamology

Take a few moments to quiet yourself before bed by turning off all distractions and taking a few deep breaths. Set an intention to remember your dreams and to use them as a way to deepen your self-understanding. Keep your notebook and pen by the side of your bed. If you wake up in the middle of the night and remember your dream, write it down immediately. (If you'd like, you can ask yourself to pick up the same dream when you go back to sleep.) In the morning, write down anything you remember about your dreams. To recall dreams, it's best to wake up naturally. An alarm tends to jolt the dream out of your memory, so this may be a good first-time exercise for a night when you don't have obligations the following morning. If you do not remember your dreams or think you have not dreamed at all, that is fine. Have no judgment, attachment, or frustration. Allow for the process to unfold by repeating this practice each night.

4

AUGUST

~~~

Suffering just means you're having a bad dream. Happiness means you're having a good dream. Enlightenment means getting out of the dream altogether.

—JED MCKENNA, *SPIRITUAL ENLIGHTENMENT: THE DAMNEDEST THING*

5

AUGUST

~~~

Deepen Sleep and Awaken Spirit

For this meditation, you will need comfortable headphones that you can sleep with. Prepare earlier in the day by finding a binaural beats meditation on YouTube, iTunes, or a meditation app that you resonate with. (See the resources on page 223 for ideas.) Binaural beats are different tones with certain frequencies playing in each ear to bring about a meditative state. Pop your headphones in and listen to the sounds while preparing for bed and/or while you drift off to sleep, to awaken your spirit and deepen your slumber.

6

AUGUST

As you go about your day, repeat this affirmation silently: "My inner guru lies within the silence."

7

AUGUST

You are the best interpreter of your own dreams. Seeking expert advice is powerful, but so many answers lie within you. Have the patience and allow for the wisdom to bubble up in your consciousness. Look at your notebook and review the dreams you've recorded the past few nights. What are they saying to you? Is there a pattern? Continue to record your dreams and revisit your notebook from time to time to find the messages and patterns.

8
AUGUST

Higher Guidance

In this exercise, you will seek advice from your Inner Knowing. Do a clearing meditation such as the "Crystal Healing Cave" from my *Journey with Guided Meditation* album to calm your mind. Set the intention of receiving guidance on a particular issue or question. Go to your computer, open a blank document in your word processor, close your eyes, and wait in the silence. When words come into your consciousness, whether in a stream or word by word, type them into the document. Don't think about the words or how they sound coming to you or if they make any sense at all. Just listen and type. Once you have stopped receiving any prompt, open your eyes and read the message. Practice this as often as you'd like to make a stronger connection to your Inner Knowing.

9
AUGUST

Today, turn to this affirmation for support: "I combine non-resistant thought and my desire along with my dedication, determination, and discipline to access limitless possibilities."

10
AUGUST

~~~

In the movie *What Dreams May Come*, many of the characters who have passed on create an existence from their mind of a time or experience that brought them infinite joy. They are not limited by what is perceived to be possible. There are characters that create unbounded despair, pain, and misery because that was in their hearts when they passed. Use your imagination to imagine an afterlife that you would create from the most precious and beautiful experiences and thoughts of your life and record them in your notebook.

11
AUGUST

~~~

Repeat this affirmation throughout your day: "There is no death. Only life and life as spiritual beings. We transition from one experience to another. This is a time of release and celebration."

12
AUGUST

~~~

Dreamscape

Find a landscape painting or photograph that speaks to you. (Choose an image from your favorite artist or see the resources on page 223.) Spend at least 5 to 10 minutes digesting every aspect of the image: the color, the texture, and the light. Close your eyes and visualize yourself inside the image. Allow yourself to interact with the scene and fully experience the location. This exercise helps you stretch your ability to dream, visualize, and imagine.

13
AUGUST

~~~

American Tibetan Buddhist Pema Chödrön has stated that "nothing ever goes away until it has taught us what we need to know." Spend some time journaling in your notebook about recurring negative patterns or dreams. Explore the messages you might be missing. To get the ball rolling, answer the following questions: Are you having a recurring dream? Are you attracting the same situation, such as abandonment or combative relationships, over and over again? What are they trying to tell you?

14
AUGUST

Today, turn to this affirmation for support: "This life is a construct, a schoolhouse, and a platform for learning. I embrace the wisdom."

15
AUGUST

Body Scan

A body scan can bring your awareness to where fear is sitting in your body, whether it's fear of limits, dreams, or success. Sit quietly, close your eyes, and breathe rhythmically in through your nose and exhale through your mouth. Visualize breathing in light and exhaling static, lower-frequency energies that block your optimal life experience. Ask yourself, "Where is there fear in my body?" Allow a visual to come to your mind's eye. It's possible a twitch or a quick pain will occur and signal the location. Honor and accept whatever message of awareness you receive. Don't resist the fear; embrace and try to understand it with compassion. As you breathe, visualize light entering that location through your breath, giving the fear permission to leave your body as the light transmutes the fear into a higher frequency of love.

16
AUGUST

Dreams are the touchstones of our character.
—HENRY DAVID THOREAU

17
AUGUST

Passion is powerful fuel. When every cell of your body dreams your dream, and you feel that there is no backup plan or other path to take, you know the passion for this dream is powered by your soul. State, "I acknowledge and honor my soul's path for the highest and best for all."

18
AUGUST

〜〜〜

Focus more on your desire than on your doubt, and the dream will take care of itself.

—MARK TWAIN

19
AUGUST

〜〜〜

When my elderly mother passed away, I was lying on my bed 3,000 miles away in a state of meditation, somewhere between awake and asleep. A very clear vision of her in her forties hovering over a stunning field of red poppies came into my mind. My heart was full, and I knew she had arrived in the afterlife. Take a few moments to quiet yourself, and ask your Higher Self to bring forth a memory that was mystical, spiritual, and felt beautiful. Jot down in your notebook how this memory gave you clarity and confirmation of something. If you cannot bring forth a memory, write an affirmative statement that you desire to have this type of experience.

20
AUGUST

~~~

Repeat this affirmation throughout the day: "The limits I impose in my mind are the only things that stifle my experience of greater awareness."

21
AUGUST

~~~

Acts of Kindness

As you navigate your day, be aware of your acts of kindness. Do they have an authentic or unauthentic motivation? For example, are you holding the door for someone out of kindness or because you desire a response of gratitude? While driving, are you letting someone go in front of you to help them out or because you want to impress them with your generosity? Are you giving to charity because it is expected or because you truly want to help? Your motivation and intention are a powerful force. Today, do three acts of kindness with the noblest of intentions and without any expectations.

22
AUGUST

~~~

Jot down a paragraph or two in your notebook about your soul's journey and purpose. Ask yourself the following questions: "What is my personal and sacred dream? Am I living someone else's dream? Am I thriving or surviving?" This prompt may ignite more journaling at this time or another as you develop a more in-depth understanding of your life's purpose.

23
AUGUST

~~~

Logic will get you from A to B. Imagination will take you everywhere.

—ALBERT EINSTEIN

24
AUGUST

Superhero

Let's play with ideas to stretch the imagination and possibilities. This exercise helps you break through limiting beliefs by visualizing yourself with the ability to fly like a superhero. Sit quietly, close your eyes, and begin to breathe rhythmically in through your nose and out through your mouth. Once your body is relaxed, envision yourself getting up from the chair. Think upward and envision yourself lifting off the ground and flying up into the sky—above the trees, the buildings, the clouds, wherever you wish to go. You may land on a rooftop and explore this elevated height to view something on the ground. When you're ready, descend back to the earth at a smooth pace and land softly. You are in full control. You can add to the visualization exercise by bringing along a partner, an angel, or a loved one to hold your hand as you fly.

25
AUGUST

Make this your mantra today: "Just because I cannot see it doesn't mean that it doesn't exist."

26
AUGUST

~~~

Ancient Greek philosopher Plato asked, "How can you prove whether at this moment we are sleeping, and all our thoughts are a dream; or whether we are awake, and talking to one another in the waking state?" Take this time to journal. Write out Plato's question and explore how it makes you feel. Does it bring consternation, fear, or anxiety to your emotional body, or does it resonate as truth?

27
AUGUST

~~~

Yes, I am a dreamer. For a dreamer is one who can find his way by moonlight, and see the dawn before the rest of the world.

—HENRY DAVID THOREAU

28
AUGUST

~~~

Repeat this affirmation throughout the day: "I dream a dream of paradise on earth, for one and all."

29
AUGUST

~~~

Take out your notebook and draw your dream of a perfect world. What does it look like to you? Hold the vision in your heart and mind. Acknowledge that change must occur; processes and negative creations must collapse for your new Earth to emerge. The same is true for your own life. What does your personal utopia look like? Draw and journal about that, too.

30
AUGUST

Carefully watch your thoughts, for they become your words. Manage and watch your words, for they will become your actions. Consider and judge your actions, for they have become your habits. Acknowledge and watch your habits, for they shall become your values. Understand and embrace your values, for they become your destiny.

—MAHATMA GANDHI

31
AUGUST

Make this your mantra today: "I love and approve of myself as I journey through this life experience."

SEPTEMBER

1
SEPTEMBER

As you go about your day, repeat this affirmation silently: "I navigate my daily experience with grace."

2
SEPTEMBER

I do not at all understand the mystery of grace—only that it meets us where we are but does not leave us where it found us.

—ANNE LAMOTT

3
SEPTEMBER

~~~

What visual do you conjure in your mind when you think of the word grace? It can be a challenging word to define as it can be more of a feeling, an essence rather than a thing. Explore the definition of grace with an Internet search and then look for examples of it in your life today. Take a moment to journal your findings and answer these questions: "Does grace reside within me? Is it a Divine force? Is there someone I know who embodies grace? How can I add more grace to my life?"

4
SEPTEMBER

~~~

Happiness cannot be traveled to, owned, earned, worn, or consumed. Happiness is the spiritual experience of living every minute with love, grace, and gratitude.

—DENIS WAITLEY

Candlelight

Find a quiet place with no music or background noise. Place a candle on a table in front of you about a foot away and light it. Quiet the mind with a few deep breaths. Now, look into the candle flame for a few moments as you contemplate the word grace. Do you see grace in the flame? Does the flame dance effortlessly? Is it peaceful? Simply be aware of the flame without judgment. When complete, extinguish the flame in gratitude.

Allow the storms of your life to pass with more ease when you dip your consciousness just below the surface of the crashing waves. The calm resides there. Make this your mantra today: "I am the calm beneath the waves."

7
SEPTEMBER

~

In your notebook, explore the idea of equanimity, an evenness of mind, in your life and how it can express itself. Ask yourself if it is possible to smooth out the significant highs and lows you may be experiencing. Are you being hypersensitive and allowing your emotions to take you for a ride on a runaway train? Acknowledge that you have full control over your own emotions and that you are not responsible for others' reactions or feelings.

8
SEPTEMBER

~

All that we are is the result of what we have thought: it is founded on our thoughts and made up of our thoughts. If a man speak or act with an evil thought, suffering follows him as the wheel follows the hoof of the beast that draws the wagon. . . . If a man speak or act with a good thought, happiness follows him like a shadow that never leaves him.

—GAUTAMA BUDDHA

9
SEPTEMBER

Silence

Today, I invite you to experience as much silence as possible. Turn off the television, the radio in your car, and the background music at home. Get comfortable with silence. It may feel uncomfortable at first as you break through the pattern of constant stimulation. Become mindfully aware of any resistance you are feeling. You can also be mindfully aware of any noises you can't do anything about. Simply notice the sounds of a car engine as it passes along your street, the ticking clock, the wind, etc., allowing the sounds to pass through your awareness without judgment, bringing you back to the gap or void of silence. If silence is already prominent in your life, explore any feelings of resistance you may have toward it and how you may be producing more isolation by your resistant approach toward it. Understanding your perception of the silence or isolation will help you embrace the now and fortify you to take responsibility to shift your mind away from resistance.

10

SEPTEMBER

~~~

Wayne Dyer is quoted saying, "When you are spiritually connected, you are not looking for occasions to be offended, and you are not judging and labeling others." In your notebook, journal your answer to the following question: "Where am I hypersensitive, easily offended, and judgmental toward others in my life?"

11

SEPTEMBER

~~~

Even a happy life cannot be without a measure of darkness, and the word happy would lose its meaning if it were not balanced by sadness. It is far better to take things as they come along with patience and equanimity.

—CARL JUNG

12
SEPTEMBER

~~~

Repeat this affirmation throughout the day: "I invoke the vibration of grace in my life. I am in the process of understanding grace more fully."

13
SEPTEMBER

~~~

Mindful Chores

A daily mindfulness practice permeates every area of your life—and, yes, that even includes chores. Let's take doing the dishes, for instance: Today, when you approach a sink full of dirty dishes, whether you are handwashing or rinsing and loading the dishwasher, I invite you to do so mindfully—meaning, slow it down. Change the perspective from one of "having to do the dishes" to a feeling of appreciation for the means by which the dishes get washed. Appreciate the fresh-smelling soap and the clean sponge. If you'd like, enjoy the memory of how you came to acquire the dishes. If you have a dishwasher, appreciate the modern convenience as you load the dishes.

14
SEPTEMBER

Make this your mantra today: "I appreciate the grace and whispers from Spirit that guide and strengthen me along my path."

15
SEPTEMBER

Social Media Freedom Day

Social media has its downsides. Some people have actually become depressed because they spend a significant amount of their time and energy focused on what others think of them through *likes* and comments. A fear of missing out has become a real thing in our social media–focused society. Perceiving that others' lives are more glamorous and celebratory can leave people feeling saddened by their own lives. Even if this phenomenon does not apply to the way you use social media, it is always good to do an evaluation and take a break from time to time. Today, I encourage you to unplug from social media. Use that time instead to connect to your Inner Self with a longer meditation.

16
SEPTEMBER

~~~

Faith consists in believing when it is beyond the power of reason to believe.

—VOLTAIRE

17
SEPTEMBER

~~~

Isolation and self-observation may feel like a safe cocoon while you are deepening your mindfulness experience, but engaging with the outside world will provide far more opportunities to practice mindfulness. Take your practice on the road and set aside some time today to interact with others without judgment. Practice being mindful both of yourself and other people during your conversations and activities.

18
SEPTEMBER

~~~

The voice of conscience is so delicate that it is easy to stifle it; but it is also so clear that it is impossible to mistake it.

—MADAME DE STAËL

19
SEPTEMBER

~~~

Today, turn to this affirmation for support: "My Inner Light is a spark of the universal grace and shines bright for the world to see."

20
SEPTEMBER

≈

Notice Five Things

Today, remind yourself to slow down and be mindfully aware of your surroundings by noticing five things that you would have missed if you were not in practice. This exercise is fabulous to add to your daily routine. It is like building the awareness muscle and will support you to become more aware with each passing day.

Yesterday, my five things were: I noticed a robin in the tree, which brought a beautiful memory of childhood to me. I experienced my cat chirping as he looked out onto the garden, and I took the moment to witness a bunny in my yard. While driving my son to school, I gifted my consciousness with the sight of the snowcapped mountains, and then we discussed our appreciation for where we live. As I entered the bank, I greeted the teller with a good morning, which she really appreciated. (You never know how your smile will impact another's day.) On the way to the store, I witnessed an awe-inspiring sunset that expanded my heart. What will you notice today?

21
SEPTEMBER

Joy has to do with seeing how big, how completely unob-
structed, and how precious things are. Resenting what
happens to you and complaining about your life are like
refusing to smell the wild roses when you go for a morning
walk, or like being so blind that you don't see a huge black
raven when it lands in the tree that you're sitting under.
We can get so caught up in our own personal pain or wor-
ries that we don't notice that the wind has come up or that
somebody has put flowers on the dining room table or that
when we walked out in the morning, the flags weren't up,
and that when we came back, they were flying.

—PEMA CHÖDRÖN,
AWAKENING LOVING-KINDNESS

22
SEPTEMBER

Repeat this affirmation: "I acknowledge every experience as
a teacher."

23
SEPTEMBER

~

Naturally Grace

Plan a 20-minute session, preferably early in the morning, to sit silently as the morning offers its own form of quiet. If you reside in a location where you can view nature, do so. Experience solitude fully in a nonresistant manner. If your life is full of solitude, I invite you to dance with nature from a place of visual engagement. Look for the elegance, beauty, and grace that seems effortless in nature. Allow for any surprises to cross your path, such as a bird, bunny, or a falling leaf. If a thought arises other than this appreciation, gently direct your awareness back to your acknowledgment of the fluidity and grace of nature.

24
SEPTEMBER

~

Today, turn to this affirmation for support: "I amplify the essence of grace from Spirit in my life."

25
SEPTEMBER
~~~

In your notebook, explore what has transpired since you first began this practice of mindfulness. What negative habitual patterns have you released? Have new, more positive and productive patterns arisen? Journal about your experiences these past nine months.

26
SEPTEMBER
~~~

Without the spiritual world the material world is a disheartening enigma.

—JOSEPH JOUBERT

27
SEPTEMBER

~~~

As you go about your day, repeat this affirmation silently: "The mystery of life is an explorative journey in which I learn to understand my soul's truth and the nature of reality."

28
SEPTEMBER

~~~

I Am Facewash

This five-minute exercise can be done daily. This thoughtful facewash is meant to connect your mindful awareness to the magnificence of your face as an expression of all your experiences and the Light that resides within. Slow down and take the time to gently nourish your face by washing with an all-natural product. With each splash of water, appreciate the deliberate and loving process of honoring your face. State in your mind or aloud: "I am comfortable in my own skin. I am a Divine expression of all my thoughts and experiences as they express on my face. My inner Light shines bright through my eyes and from my face."

29
SEPTEMBER

~~~

Pope Francis is quoted as saying, "Grace is not part of consciousness; it is the amount of light in our souls, not knowledge nor reason." Write this quote in your notebook and explore it more fully through journaling. What does your "Soul's Light" or "Inner Light" mean to you?

30
SEPTEMBER

~~~

Everyone is special, and no one is more special. The whole of humanity is a mass expression of experience. Today, repeat this affirmation: "Each one of us is a manifestation of Light."

OCTOBER

1
OCTOBER

Acceptance looks like a passive state, but in reality it brings something entirely new into this world. That peace, a subtle energy vibration, is consciousness.

—ECKHART TOLLE

2
OCTOBER

The "what is" (meaning, what is happening in your life right now) is often given a bad rap. In your notebook, explore all the areas of your life: health, work, love, spirituality, relationships, and any other areas you can think of. Connect to your thoughts with mindful awareness in nonjudgment. Can you accept where you are right now as the perfection that it is? Being aware of "what is," and accepting it for what it is, allows you to create something new based on that wisdom, if what you are experiencing is not what you desire.

3
OCTOBER

~~~

Make this your mantra today: "Spirit is always orchestrating for my highest good."

4
OCTOBER

~~~

Be a Voice

Have you become too complacent and quiet? Are you holding back from expressing yourself? Albert Einstein said, "Be a voice, not an echo." I have that saying on my bedroom wall. It reminds me to not be afraid of who I am, to express my own style and personal message, and to honor it as my individual expression in the world. Today, step into your personal expression as though no one is watching, and enjoy it. Wear two different-colored socks, a silly hat, or crazy glasses if that is your thing. Listen to opera at work, dance to disco, or rap to your favorite hip-hop jam in the car. Crack the door of your individuality and let it out for a spin.

5
OCTOBER

~~~

As you go about your day, repeat this affirmation silently: "Right now, I honor that I am in the perfect scenario for my growth and expansion."

6
OCTOBER

~~~

Author Alan Watts spoke of Buddha's doctrine: "Man suffers because of his craving to possess and keep forever things which are essentially impermanent . . . this frustration of the desire to possess is the immediate cause of suffering." In your notebook, journal about the ways you are suffering. Does it have to do with your yearning to hold on to or control something or someone? Nothing is permanent; change is a natural course of life. Could it be time to surrender to change and see what happens? Ask your Inner Knowing.

7
OCTOBER

I believe that everything happens for a reason. People change so that you can learn to let go, things go wrong so that you appreciate them when they're right, you believe lies so you eventually learn to trust no one but yourself, and sometimes good things fall apart so better things can fall together.

—MARILYN MONROE

8
OCTOBER

Self-Acceptance Breath

Breathe in through your nose and exhale through your mouth. With each deepening breath, begin to relax your body. After several breaths, envision a soft white light about six inches in front of your forehead. Connect with this light and keep breathing in and out. State three times: "I accept myself and love myself for the perfect creation that I am."

9
OCTOBER

〜

You cannot find any peace by escaping from human pain and suffering; you have to find peace and harmony right in the midst of human pain. That is the purpose of spiritual life.

—DAININ KATAGIRI

10
OCTOBER

〜

Look at where you may be tricking yourself into acceptance by just "keeping the peace." You may be neglecting your inner voice and gut feelings. Journal about this in your notebook: Are you fooling yourself into acceptance when that acceptance is really silencing your Inner Knowing? Do you feel numb to your life experience?

11
OCTOBER

~~~

Today, turn to this affirmation for support: "I meet life's challenges with mindful awareness."

12
OCTOBER

~~~

Class Act

Isolation can happen for many reasons, and before you know it, you may have lost the feeling of community. Loneliness can creep in. If this is the case for you, it's time to reengage. Take a class! It may feel scary or intimidating at first, but it will be great once you shake off the dust of seclusion. Try taking a meditation class. It supports your mindfulness practice and you will engage with others of like mind. Today, search your local community center, ask around for a wellness or spiritual shop, or join Meetup.com and explore a plethora of classes.

13
OCTOBER

~~~

Review your recent experiences and explore what might have caused you to worry. Would those things have been resolved whether you worried or not? Dale Carnegie said, "Remember, today is the tomorrow you worried about yesterday." Journal in your notebook with this prompt: Does worry ever change the outcome of a situation?

14
OCTOBER

~~~

Repeat this affirmation throughout the day: "Worry limits my personal power and so I accept the flow of life."

15
OCTOBER

~

Happiness and freedom begin with one principle. Some things are within your control and some are not.

—EPICTETUS

16
OCTOBER

~

Massage

Today, spend some time massaging your hands, feet, and legs the way you would envision a professional would do it. Better yet, if possible, book a professional massage. Honoring yourself through self-care in this way supports your mind, body, and spirit. Going for professional massages has been one of the best decisions in my personal self-care regimen. There are many franchise outlets that provide massage at a discounted rate based on membership, such as Massage Envy, Massage Heights, and Hand & Stone Massage and Facial Spa. You can also explore discount coupons such as Groupon for your local spa.

17
OCTOBER

~

Make this your mantra today: "As I nourish myself mindfully, I am better equipped to support others."

18
OCTOBER

~

Criticizing and disparaging yourself does not serve you. Has that pattern supported you thus far? Has it helped you be better in any way? In this journaling session, write down the areas in which you disrespect yourself with self-deprecating and criticizing comments. Then create a new program of internal dialogue that includes self-approval and acceptance. Start with, "I love and approve of myself. I am perfect in my imperfections. I am more than enough."

19
OCTOBER

~~~

Sit in the Sun

I love the sun! I live in Las Vegas, so I guess I'd better. In the sunlight,
I access renewal, whether direct or in the illuminated path it takes within
my home. I feel vibrant and refreshed, as if it feeds my soul. If the sun is
shining today, take five minutes (bundle yourself up if it is cold) and sit
quietly where the sun is shining on you. Close your eyes and allow the sun
to nourish your soul with the brilliance of its light on your face. If you feel
the need for sunscreen, by all means apply it. If you prefer to sit near a
window for the diffused sunlight, that's okay, too. No thoughts, just appreciation for the sun and the warmth and nourishment it provides.

20
OCTOBER

~~~

**Life is a series of natural and spontaneous changes.
Don't resist them; that only creates sorrow. Let reality
be reality. Let things flow naturally forward in whatever
way they like.**

—LAOZI

21
OCTOBER

~~~

When you navigate life mindfully, you'll find every step of the journey is an opportunity that gifts you what you desire. It may appear to be something else, but when you think on it, you can see the hidden opportunities. In your notebook, write down situations you declined that could have been doors opening for you. What have you said no to when an opportunity presented itself? Dream and write down what could have happened if you had accepted. Then, add when you accepted a path that led to something amazing and magical. Did you follow an inner voice, an instinct that guided you?

22
OCTOBER

~~~

By letting go, it all gets done.

—LAOZI

23

~~~

Cultivate Compassion

Sit quietly and allow your mind to settle on three basic needs of life: food, shelter, and clothing. With each topic, explore your own existence and how appreciative you are for your current situation. Even if your situation is not optimal, and you may want to change it or elevate it, meet your thoughts where you are now in appreciation compared with those who are less fortunate. For example, as you address your need for food, you may want to purchase organic produce but cannot afford to do so right now. However, you do have food to eat, and there are many who have far less than you. So, always bring yourself back to feelings of gratitude for having enough. You may want to do an Internet search on poverty or explore charities and websites that report on food scarcity and depriva- tion in the world. Do this same exercise for housing/shelter and clothing. Take this opportunity to donate to those charities. Always return to the feelings of gratitude for your life experience. Quietly contemplating those who are less fortunate will cultivate compassion.

24
OCTOBER

~

Until you are happy with who you are, you will never be happy with what you have.

—ZIG ZIGLAR

25
OCTOBER

~

With mindful awareness, explore the contents of your wardrobe. Look through it all: every hanger and each pair of shoes. Are there items that still have tags on them? Are there things you've never worn? How much of what you have do you wear regularly? One way we try to fill an emotional and spiritual void is through acquiring stuff. Take a personal inventory of your life. Get your notebook and ask yourself, "Where am I projecting outwardly through material goods my desire to fill my soul?" If your closet is sparse, explore where else in your life you may be projecting outwardly the need to fill your inner world. Some examples might be needing the latest and greatest technology even though your current device is perfectly fine, collecting things, and always keeping busy.

26
OCTOBER
~~~

In the Closet

It's time to clean out your closet. The feeling of liberation and freedom is monumental when you shed the items you purchased from a subconscious motive of filling an emotional void. This is a great opportunity to donate to your favorite charity. Explore which charities in your local area will accept clothing donations; some charities may even pick up your items. If not your closet, choose another area of your home where you've accumulated a lot of stuff, and give each item your mindful attention to decide whether or not it is a keeper from a place of emotional fullness.

27
OCTOBER
~~~

Make this your mantra today: "I fill my emotional and spiritual body with love and light."

28
OCTOBER

~~~

No one can make you feel inferior without your consent.

—ELEANOR ROOSEVELT

29
OCTOBER

~~~

Being comfortable in your own skin is freedom. Mark Twain said, "The worst loneliness is not to be comfortable with yourself." In your notebook, jot down ways that you are not comfortable in your own skin. Reflect on whether or not this has led to loneliness, isolation, or living inauthentically.

30
OCTOBER

~~

Does the statement "People treat me the way I allow them to treat me" resonate with you? Your experiences often reflect how you feel about yourself. Repeat to yourself often: "As I grow mindfully, I attract more compassion in my life. I respectfully and lovingly honor myself on this awakened path."

31
OCTOBER

~~

Read, recite, and repeat: "My past experiences do not label me a failure or loser but rather a triumphant spiritual warrior making my way through the forest of duality experience."

NOVEMBER

Kindness

Sit comfortably, close your eyes, and take a few deep breaths. Now visualize a pet that you have fond feelings toward. This pet may have passed on, or it may be your current fur baby. If you never had a pet, imagine one you think you would like: a puppy or a kitten, or any animal you could potentially cuddle with. Since this is an exercise for your imagination, you can even choose a wild animal such as a bear or a wildcat, but in this case, the animal is tame and loving. Now envision this animal in your arms or lap, completely surrendered and emotionally connected with you. They feel safe and secure in your arms, and they respond by nuzzling you or purring. Take a few moments to interact with and communicate your feelings of love and kindness toward this precious animal that has full faith in you. Once you have connected on this level of feeling kindness toward this animal, you can release the vision and set the intention to treat animals and humans alike with the same kindness.

2

NOVEMBER

〜〜

There are many things to be grateful for, such as our entire human experience, the planet, and every possible element that makes this world what it is. Take a few moments to thoroughly ponder your life thus far. What are you most grateful for in your overall life experience? Think about and journal on one expression of your gratitude.

3

NOVEMBER

〜〜

Appreciation is a wonderful thing: It makes what is excellent in others belong to us as well.

—VOLTAIRE

4
NOVEMBER

~~~

So Funny!

Charlie Chaplin said, "A day without laughter is a day wasted." Let's not waste this one! Right now, laugh—even if you can only muster a little giggle to prime the pump. Then get louder. Force the laughter if you must. Practice laughing until it feels authentic and exuberant. Now, throughout the rest of your day, find opportunities to laugh. Laugh at yourself, at the antics of a dog or cat, at a funny meme. Be aware of what brings laughter to your lips. At day's end, express gratitude that you have so much to laugh about. However, even if you cannot find something to laugh about, you can still laugh. (See the resources on page 223 to check out Laughter Yoga International.)

5
NOVEMBER

~~~

Today, turn to this affirmation for support: "I understand that any less-than-optimal life experience is happening for me not to me."

Notice Anger

Any emotion that controls you and moves you from your state of peace and well-being is a metaphorical prison for your spirit. So, how do you free yourself? Awareness, time, and breath are good places to start. When you feel an angry feeling welling up, or if it leaps out as an outburst before you become aware, take time to step away. That may or may not be a physical step away, but give yourself time to breathe and allow the feelings and thoughts to settle. There's no judgment of yourself or others, just awareness of the emotion. Breathe as you would when preparing for meditation, deeply expanding your chest and belly. Allow the resonance of anger to shed from your being. What have you learned? What would you do differently next time? The Universe *will* give you another opportunity to practice, so it is best to take the time to work through the lesson and how you will approach a similar situation for a more mindful and optimal result.

7

Searching for sage advice in life is a wonderful way to move along your path. Maybe you've been a seeker for a long time and have engaged with coaches or received spiritual support. Maybe you are newly beginning your journey. Either way, reflect on your life and journal in your notebook. When in your life experience has a teacher, guide, or guru shown up for you at the perfect time to provide wisdom? How did you benefit from the advice?

8

NOVEMBER

Through the eyes of gratitude, everything is a miracle.

—MARY DAVIS

9
NOVEMBER

~~~

Gratitude Journal

Being grateful is a positive feeling, but not everyone is taught to be grateful for the little things that happen every day. Today, start a new journal just for this purpose and title it your "Gratitude Journal." Every night before you go to bed, write down three things that happened that day for which you are thankful. Review the day meticulously and enjoy your awareness of the gifts the day brought—for example, the sun was shining, there was no line at the bank, your friend surprised you with a visit, or you finished a project at work.

10
NOVEMBER

~~~

Make being mindful of your alignment with Spirit, or the highest non-physical power, a daily pattern and habit. In your notebook, write down your thoughts on the following: What does "highest nonphysical power" mean to you? Explore what this alignment feels like to you. Does it feel like bliss? Love? Peace?

11
NOVEMBER

~~~

I will love the light for it shows me the way, yet I will endure the darkness because it shows me the stars.

—OG MANDINO

12
NOVEMBER

~~~

Starry, Starry Night

Stephen Hawking said, "Look up at the stars and not down at your feet. Try to make sense of what you see and wonder about what makes the universe exist. Be curious." With this in mind, find a place where you can go to see the stars. It might be your own backyard, or you might have to go a little farther. If so, make an event out of it. Grab a thermos of hot cocoa, take a car ride, and be amazed by what you see in the night sky.

13
NOVEMBER

~~~

The pineal gland is a small pea-sized gland within the endocrine system that produces melatonin (aka the sleep hormone). It is located deep in the center of the brain and is often called the third eye. There is far more to this little pinecone-shaped beauty than science would suggest; it is associated with our intuitive ability, spirituality, and human potential. (See page 223 for a link to a Gaia post on the pineal gland and the third eye chakra.) Once you've read the article, explore your answer to this question in your notebook: "Am I fully expressing my highest human potential?"

14
NOVEMBER

~~~

Make this your mantra today: "I am grateful for the earth, the sky, the sun, the moon, the land, the trees, and all the beautiful flowers on the planet."

15
NOVEMBER

~~~

Pine Cone Mania

Some areas of Earth are inundated with pine cones. If you take a walk in the woods, you may witness a sea of them on the ground. I've had a fascination with pine cones ever since I was a child. To this day, I will bring home the perfect pine cone I find on my walk. Now it's your turn. If you live in an area where pine cones are abundant, go out and find yourself your own perfect pine cone. If you don't live in an area with pine cones, visit your local craft store or search for them online.

16
NOVEMBER

~~~

The struggle ends when gratitude begins.

—NEALE DONALD WALSCH

17
NOVEMBER

~~~

As you go about your day, repeat this affirmation silently: "I am a cocreator with the Divine Spirit. I am never alone."

18
NOVEMBER

~~~

As we express our gratitude, we must never forget that the highest appreciation is not to utter words, but to live by them.

—JOHN F. KENNEDY

19
NOVEMBER
~~~

There are many people who are unhappy, desperate for help, and completely stuck. However, when it comes down to it, some people are not willing to do what it takes to change. To turn things around, you need to practice self-observation and self-reliance and take responsibility for the inner work. In your notebook, explore these questions: "Do I take responsibility for my life experience?" "Do I play the victim and use others as a scapegoat in order to receive sympathy?" "Am I committed to the inner work?"

20
NOVEMBER
~~~

Repeat this affirmation throughout the day: "I create my new reality by gradual change through daily habits."

21
NOVEMBER

~

In the Shade

In the Gaia TV series *Initiation,* host Matías De Stefano provides a wonderful analogy about the real meaning of compassion. He says, "Trees don't bend to assist other trees that fell down. They don't lift another tree up. They share all the energy so they can transform from that experience." Compassion is not pity. Your job is to be in alignment with yourself, your heart, and your Spirit. By this act, you will raise up the whole. Today, locate the most spectacular tree you can find and sit under it for 20 minutes in silence. Allow the tree to communicate with you through thoughts, feelings, and images, and send back loving energy.

22
NOVEMBER

~

One of my favorite things to say to myself and clients is "Gratitude is the fertilizer for your dreams." In your notebook, journal your answer to this question: "When in my life have I been the most grateful?"

23
NOVEMBER

~

Gratitude is not only the greatest of virtues but the parent of all others.

—CICERO

24
NOVEMBER

~

Today, turn to this affirmation for support: "I am always provided for and all my needs are met."

25
NOVEMBER

~~~

Empathy, compassion, and sympathy are wonderful traits. When someone you know is struggling, it's challenging to not take on their burden or want to fix the situation. With mindfulness awareness, ask yourself if the help or assistance you want to provide will benefit them for their highest good. Sometimes, by saving another, you rob them of the opportunity to grow. Sometimes, it's perfectly supportive to step in and lend a hand. Make sure you check in with your Inner Knowing and ask, "Is this the best thing for all involved?" In your notebook, explore this topic by writing about the times you were helped that positively supported your growth and the times when help hindered your growth.

26
NOVEMBER

~~~

Before you consume any meal or drink, repeat this affirmation silently: "I am grateful for this nourishment." This affirmation vibrationally elevates the nourishment and allows you to become more aware of what you are putting in your body as a sacred practice.

27
NOVEMBER

~~~

Gratitude, like faith, is a muscle. The more you use it, the stronger it grows, and the more power you have to use it on your behalf. If you do not practice gratefulness, its benefaction will go unnoticed, and your capacity to draw on its gifts will be diminished. To be grateful is to find blessings in everything. This is the most powerful attitude to adopt, for there are blessings in everything.

—ALAN COHEN

28
NOVEMBER

~~~

Read, recite, and repeat: "I do not close my heart due to past experiences, as that would deprive the world of my love."

29
NOVEMBER

Singing Bowls

One of my favorite relaxing sounds is a singing bowl. I use crystal bowls in my practice, but the Tibetan metal bowls also have a lovely tone. Meditating while listening to the bowls is known to help depression, anxiety, stress, and much more. Today, explore YouTube for a singing bowl session that feels right to you. (See the resources on page 223 for my recommendation.) You can play this in the background all day as you go about your normal routine or play it during meditation for as long as you desire.

30
NOVEMBER

Don't pray when it rains if you don't pray when the sun shines.

—LEROY "SATCHEL" PAIGE

DECEMBER

1
DECEMBER

~

Make this your mantra today: "Peace and love dwell within me."

2
DECEMBER

~

We cannot give what we do not have: We cannot bring peace to the world if we ourselves are not peaceful. We cannot bring love to the world if we ourselves are not loving. Our true gift to ourselves and others lies not in what we have but in who we are.

—MARIANNE WILLIAMSON

3
DECEMBER

Peacefully Crafted

It is the intention behind a symbol that makes it powerful for good or bad—if we were to judge it. Today, focus on the peace symbol. (See the resources on page 223 to learn more about this symbol.) Even if you do not consider yourself crafty, there are simple creative projects that can emphasize peace within your environment. Doodle the peace symbol on your calendar, notebook, or a sticky note as a reminder to affirm peace in your life. You can also paint the symbol on an object such as a rock or a T-shirt, or sketch it on a pad and frame it. However you wish to use the symbol for this exercise will be perfect.

4
DECEMBER

We can never obtain peace in the outer world until we make peace with ourselves.

—DALAI LAMA XIV

5
DECEMBER
〜〜

Kindness cannot be overrated. Plato said, "Be kind, for everyone you meet is fighting a harder battle." Over the years, I have coached some incredible souls managing deep levels of suffering. You wouldn't know it just by looking at them. Maybe the person driving too slowly or the person who cut you off wasn't the jerk you thought them to be. They could have been distracted by gargantuan issues. In your notebook, journal about this topic. Use these questions to help: How can you be kinder and more patient? When driving, for example, is there anything you can do to remind yourself that others on the road may be dealing with tough issues and give them the benefit of the doubt?

6
DECEMBER
〜〜

Today, turn to this affirmation for support: "I do not overload my days with doingness, so that I may experience more beingness."

7
DECEMBER

~

Many conflicts arise due to a lack of communication, sometimes an inner communication with oneself. Perhaps a conflict arose because you did not give enough attention to your inner dialogue. Journal about your thoughts surrounding a conflict, not to rehash it but to see it from a place of mindful awareness in nonjudgment. Afterward, notice if you feel lighter and more resolved.

8
DECEMBER

~

Book Run

Take a minute to sit quietly. Set an intention to find a special book that has a message for you. Ask this book to be clearly known to you, then take a trip to a bookstore. When there, connect with your Inner Knowing and ask to be guided to the book. Walk the aisles slowly, and with mindful attention, feel the yes or the no vibration in your body. Once you have found the bookshelf, peruse the books. Don't have any expectations or attachment; let the book come to you. Have fun and play with this process to strengthen the book's signal.

9
DECEMBER

~

Peace can only survive when fed peace.

—KIERRA C. T. BANKS

10
DECEMBER

~

"Geese are white, crows are black. No argument will change this," said Laozi. This quote reminds me how often we threaten our peace by arguing about our viewpoint. In your notebook, explore the times when you compromised your peace in order to have the last word or to be acknowledged. How has that served you? The need to be right at the cost of your own peace and well-being is an aspect of yourself to explore in this prompt. This is not about swallowing your opinion or shoving down the emotion, as such a process is detrimental to your health. Express yourself in a mindful way, and once expressed, you have released the energy of the opinion.

11
DECEMBER

~~~

As you go about your day, repeat this affirmation silently: "I see good in all people. I see good in all experiences. And so it is."

12
DECEMBER

~~~

A Letter of Praise

As the year is winding up, it's a good time to reflect and plan. Write a letter to yourself praising yourself for the amazing shifts that have occurred to bring you to where you are today. Rather than thinking of what you accomplished in the material world, think of what has transpired in your emotions and your spirit. Congratulate yourself for taking responsibility for making daily shifts. After you've written this letter, write the numbers of the approaching new year below your sign-off. Journal about what the new year will bring as you continue your mindfulness practice. Conclude with the words "I AM and So It Is" to seal your intention.

13
DECEMBER

~~~

Do you ever feel as though you are being bounced around like a pinball? If your life is filled with drama and chaos, it is a reflection of what is going on inside you. Grab your notebook and list the areas of your life that hold conflict and drama. Detail any past experiences over your lifetime that felt similar. Is there a common thread?

14
DECEMBER

~~~

Make this your mantra today: "I honor the trinity of all creation, including my mind, body, and spirit."

15
DECEMBER

～～

What can you do to promote world peace? Go home and love your family.

—MOTHER TERESA

16
DECEMBER

～～

A Year in Review

Whether you are nearing the end of a calendar year or the daily journey of this book on another timeline, give yourself time now to reflect in more depth. Journal about the shifts that occurred during this exploration of self-awareness and observation. This exercise is a bit deeper than the December 12 exercise. Move through the notebook(s) you used as the companion to this book and reread your passages. I carve out time in December of every year for this exercise as a way to remember, honor, and give thanks for the experiences and growth that unfolded throughout the year. Remember to include all the contrast that guided you beautifully to experience a different perspective.

17
DECEMBER

~

As you go about your day, repeat this affirmation silently: "I am aware of my thoughts and words and deliberately create the life I desire."

18
DECEMBER

~

When there is so much turmoil in the world, it is easy to take sides, desire to do something, and fight against the terror. Mother Teresa once wisely said, "I was once asked why I don't participate in antiwar demonstrations. I said that I will never do that, but as soon as you have a pro-peace rally, I'll be there." Putting energy toward what you do not want will not produce the result you desire. In your notebook, jot down three things you can do to promote love and peace instead of hatred and war.

19
DECEMBER

~~~

Today, turn to this affirmation for support: "I do not engage in conversations, exchanges, or experiences that hinder my vibration."

20
DECEMBER

~~~

Mother Earth

Find a photo of Earth from space that resonates with you. Look at it throughout the day, each time stating your gratitude for something that Earth provides for humanity. Like a mother nurturing her children, the planet provides for us in so many ways—food, plants, and water, to name just a few. Throughout the day, you will feel your appreciation for and awareness of Mother Earth, or Gaia, growing. Also become aware of all the ways humanity has disrespected Mother Earth, and silently communicate your apology to nature. Acknowledge that we have been blind to her consciousness, and vow to take responsibility for her care from now on.

21
DECEMBER

~~~

Mahatma Gandhi said, "Man's nature is not essentially evil. Brute nature has been known to yield to the influence of love. You must never despair of human nature." We must practice love and kindness daily even though we may not immediately witness the result of this infused positive emotion. We must be mindfully aware that the seed has been planted. In your notebook, reflect on a situation that you are currently dealing with, and instead of feeling intense negative emotions toward the situation, come at it from a different perspective with the understanding that the other person is just like you. This person is dealing with their own inner dialogue, fears, and self-image. Explore through journaling how this person is like you. Send love to the individual and the situation and ask for energetic healing. Sending love will diffuse the built-up negative energy around it.

22
DECEMBER

~

Repeat this affirmation: "I am in awe of all that I have learned and accomplished. I am in awe of all the ways I have expressed my love for myself and others."

23
DECEMBER

~

It is possible I never learned the names of birds in order to discover the bird of peace, the bird of paradise, the bird of the soul, the bird of desire. It is possible I avoided learning the names of composers and their music the better to close my eyes and listen to the mystery of all music as an ocean. It may be I have not learned dates in history in order to reach the essence of timelessness. It may be I never learned geography the better to map my own routes and discover my own lands. The unknown was my compass. The unknown was my encyclopedia. The unnamed was my science and progress.

—ANAÏS NIN

24
DECEMBER

~

Reflection

At this point in your mindfulness practice, you know that noodling relent-lessly about something negative does not serve you. That does not mean relentless noodling will not happen from time to time, so continue to practice being aware with nonjudgment. Today, reflect for five minutes on a situation that needs guidance or resolution, perhaps one that you have been turning around in your mind. Set the intention that you desire to find a resolution with ease and grace. After you have set this intention, move into a short meditation. Give thanks, knowing that the resolution is at hand—and surrender.

25
DECEMBER

~

Learn silence. With the quiet serenity of a meditative mind, listen, absorb, transcribe, and transform.

—PYTHAGORAS

26
DECEMBER

~~~

There is no shortcut to professional success or spiritual development. You must put the time in and do the work. Journal using this prompt: "Am I seeking a shortcut to the most relevant journey of my life and the exploration within?"

27
DECEMBER

~~~

Peace is not absence of conflict; it is the ability to handle conflict by peaceful means.

—RONALD REAGAN

28
DECEMBER

~~~

Repeat this affirmation throughout the day: "I review and revere all experiences of the past year as the experiment of my life unfolding."

29
DECEMBER

~~~

Through what lens do you see the world? What about other people? How do you see your relationships? Your intimate partner? Do you view new potential relationships from the eyes of the past? Spend a few minutes journaling your responses to these questions in your notebook.

30
DECEMBER

~~~

Unalome

The unalome is a symbol from the Buddhist tradition that signifies the path to enlightenment. It is a simple yet profound representation of a life on a spiritual quest. It starts with a spiral as one comes into the world, wandering and figuring things out. The spiral leads to switchback figure eights of contrast and suffering that people go through to gain wisdom and knowledge before rising in a straight-line path to the top where enlightenment is attained. In your notebook or on a fresh piece of paper, draw your own unalome that represents your life. Where are you along the pathway? (See the resources on page 223 to explore unalome.)

31
DECEMBER

~~~

When the student is ready the teacher will appear. When the student is truly ready . . . The teacher will Disappear.

—TAO TE CHING

Resources

JANUARY 22
More assistance on this prompt can be found in my online coaching programs "Mindful Makeovers" and "A Year of Living MindfulLee" leepapa.com/coaching.

JANUARY 23
Waterfall Chakra Wash by Lee Papa can be found on leepapa.com/meditation, the InsightTimer app, and here: insig.ht/gm_796. This meditation is six minutes. A longer version is available on *The Temple of All Knowing Chakra Meditation* album, and a revised version is available on *Journey with Guided Meditation* album, both by Lee Papa.

FEBRUARY 2
Read the article "The Opposite of Love Is Not Hate, It's Fear" on Exploringyourmind .com: exploringyourmind.com/opposite-love-not-hate-fear.

FEBRUARY 6
Download my free book *The Roadmap to Living Mindfully: Understanding Self-Love, Self-Care and Self-Mastery* at leepapa.com or livemindfullee.com.

FEBRUARY 12
"Relaxing River Sounds—Peaceful Forest River—Nature Video" is available on YouTube and can be found here: youtube.com/watch?v=IvjMgVS6kng&feature=youtu.be.

"Clearing by the River" meditation track can be found on the *Journey with Guided Meditation* album by Lee Papa. leepapa.com/product/the-temple-of-all-knowing -chakra-meditation.

FEBRUARY 16
For mountain pose step-by-step instructions, visit yogajournal.com/poses/mountain-pose.

Learn more about embracing change in the Mindful Makeovers online program available on leepapa.com/coaching.

MARCH 6
Guided meditations can be accessed online as mp3 downloads and CDs. A Year of Living Mindfullee is a 12-month subscription program that guides you through a supplemental process, available on leepapa.com/coaching.

MARCH 9
To explore chakras more in depth, check out *The Temple of All Knowing Chakra Meditation* album by Lee Papa and the audio program Connect Your Inner and Outer World Mindfully Through Chakra Awareness & Cleansing, by visiting leepapa.com.

MARCH 31
The exercise described is included in the Mindful Makeovers online program available on leepapa.com/coaching.

APRIL 16
To explore free meditations and a sampling of Lee Papa's collection of meditations, check out InsightTimer. Go to insighttimer.com/leepapa and explore *The Temple of All Knowing Chakra Meditation* album by Lee Papa and *Journey with Guided Meditation* by Lee Papa on leepapa.com/meditation.

The Soul Matrix, Steve Nobel's YouTube channel, offers some fabulous meditations. In the YouTube search bar, type "Steve Nobel."

MAY 8
To explore Lee Papa's sampling of meditations on InsightTimer, go to insighttimer.com/leepapa. Check out the *The Temple of All Knowing Chakra Meditation* album. Check out the *Journey with Guided Meditation* album and Storybook Meditation Series by Lee Papa on leepapa.com/meditation.

The Soul Matrix, Steve Nobel's YouTube channel, offers some fabulous meditations. In the YouTube search bar, type "Steve Nobel."

In the YouTube search bar, type "binaural beat meditations" and find one you like.

MAY 15

For more information on Young Living Essential Oils visit myyl.com/leepapa.

For comprehensive guidance on using essential oils, consult the *Essential Oils Desk Reference* available at discoverlsp.com/8th-edition-essential-oils-desk-reference.html and the *Essential Oils Integrative Medical Guide* available at discoverlsp.com/essential -oils-integrative-medical-guide.html.

MAY 18

For relaxing instrumental piano compositions, type "Louis Colaiannia" or "Giorgio Costantini" in the YouTube search bar and visit their websites at louismusic.com and pianopianoforte.com.

MAY 20

For guidance on stretching, visit stretchcoach.com/articles/how-to-stretch.

JUNE 1

The Sound of the Planets—"Alba Mundi"—by Giorgio Costantini is a wonderful piece of music for this particular meditation. You can find it here: youtube.com/watch?v =8W0mMzoZzWc or by searching the title in the YouTube search bar.

JUNE 18

Waterfall Chakra Wash by Lee Papa can be found here on leepapa.com/meditation and via InsightTimer: insig.ht/gm_796. This meditation is six minutes. A longer version is available on *The Temple of All Knowing Chakra Meditation* album by Lee Papa, and a revised version is available on *Journey with Guided Meditation* album by Lee Papa.

JULY 11

For more on the shadow self, read the article "Carl Jung and the Shadow: The Hidden Power of Our Dark Side" on academyofideas.com. You can find it here: academyofideas .com/2015/12/carl-jung-and-the-shadow-the-hidden-power-of-our-dark-side.

JULY 13

Journey on a Cloud by Lee Papa. A short version of "Journey on a Cloud" is available on leepapa.com/meditation and InsightTimer. You can find it here: insig.ht/gm_27278.

The entire text of Kahlil Gibran's *The Prophet* is available online. Visit the-prophet.com, scroll through the table of contents, and click on the chapter "On Freedom" to read the full chapter.

AUGUST 5

To explore Lee Papa's sampling of meditations on InsightTimer, go to insighttimer.com/leepapa, and check out Lee Papa's single tracks and albums. *The Temple of All Knowing Chakra Meditation* album, *Journey with Guided Meditation* album, and Storybook Meditation Series are available on leepapa.com/meditation.

In the YouTube search bar, type "Whole Body Regeneration—Full Body Healing" or follow this link: youtu.be/hdmvMc7TZn0.

In the YouTube search bar, type "The Deepest Healing Sleep REM Sleep Music Binaural Beats" or follow this link: youtu.be/xsfyb1pStdw.

AUGUST 12

Didier Ciambra is a photographic artist with an amazing gallery of images. View his landscape photos here: ciambraphotography.com/LANDSCAPES.

Jeff Oldham paints incredible nature images. You can view his paintings here: oldhamart.com.

NOVEMBER 4

You can learn more about Laughter Yoga by visiting laughteryoga.org.

NOVEMBER 13

Read the article "The Pineal Gland and the Third Eye Chakra" on gaia.com. You can find it here: gaia.com/article/pineal-third-eye-chakra.

NOVEMBER 29

In the YouTube search bar, type "Tibetan Healing Sounds—Singing Bowls—Natural Sounds Gold for Meditation & Relaxation" or follow this link: youtu.be/OW7TH2U4hps.

DECEMBER 3

To learn about the origins of the peace sign, visit peaceday.org/pcsign.htm.

DECEMBER 30

Learn more about the unalome symbol on leepapa.com/blog.

References

FEBRUARY 2

Exploring Your Mind. "The Opposite of Love Is Not Hate, It's Fear." March 6, 2016. Accessed January 21, 2020. exploringyourmind.com/opposite-love-not-hate-fear.

FEBRUARY 3

Emoto, Masaru. *The Hidden Messages in Water*. Hillsboro, OR: Beyond Words Publishing, Inc., 2004.

Hawkins, David R. "Map of Consciousness." Heartcom.org. Accessed January 21, 2020. heartcom.org/ConsciousnessScale.jpg.

FEBRUARY 10

Hicks, Esther and Jerry. *Ask and It Is Given: Learning to Manifest Your Desires.* Carlsbad, CA: Hay House, Inc., 2004.

FEBRUARY 16

Yoga Journal editors. "Mountain Pose." *Yoga Journal.* May 15, 2017. Accessed January 21, 2020. yogajournal.com/poses/mountain-pose.

MARCH 24

Nagdeve, Meenakshi. "10 Impressive Benefits of Laughter." Organic Facts. January 2, 2020. Accessed January 23, 2020. organicfacts.net/health-benefits/other/health-benefits-of-laughter.html.

MAY 24

Hay, Louise. *You Can Heal Your Life*. Carlsbad, CA: Hay House, Inc., 1984.

JUNE 5

Papa, Lee. *The Temple of All Knowing*. Lansing, MI; Light Source Publishing, 2014.

NOVEMBER 13

You and Your Hormones. "Pineal Gland." Accessed January 21, 2020.
    yourhormones.info/glands/pineal-gland.

NOVEMBER 29

Dangeli, Jevon. "Tibetan Singing Bowls—The Ancient Brain Entrainment Methodology
    for Healing and Meditation." Accessed January 24, 2020. jevondangeli.com/tibetan
    -singing-bowls-the-ancient-brain-entrainment-methodology-for-healing-and
    -meditation.

Acknowledgments

How does one sufficiently thank all those who have touched their life, influenced and impacted it in large and small ways? For me, the answer is not adequately enough. Writing these acknowledgments was more challenging than I expected because I found that I wanted to thank everyone who has ever crossed my path in this glorious experience of life. And that wasn't practical. So, I decided to mainly focus on those who were most present during the writing of this book.

My deep gratitude goes to everyone on the publishing team at Callisto Media. Your expertise, attention to detail, and authentic caring manner have been a beautiful gift. It has been a complete and utter joy to write this book with you. From acquisitions and editing to art and illustration, the experience could not have been better. Thank you for bringing to life what was created in my heart to share with the world. Special thanks to Claire Yee, my editor, for your kindness, gentle guidance, and skill on the original manuscript and Joe Cho for your thoughtfulness and patience during initial communications.

To my son. Luca, you are my great inspiration. My reason. My wisest teacher. And I am so very proud of how you navigate your personal experience of life. You are the most profound joy of my earthly walk. The journey with you stretches me and has provided such wisdom and knowledge through understanding this love. My heart expands daily being your mom. Thank you!

To my treasured friend Zulma Nieves. I cherish our friendship and our voyage together whether near or far. Thank you for your encouragement, wise words, and always seeing a greater vision than the one I have held for myself. It usually involves a yacht. LOL. Thank you for being my beautiful cheerleader. Your exuberance for life is contagious!

To my dear Samantha Segal. You are a perfect gift. Loving. Encouraging. Unfailing. Supportive. Generous. Funny! And the person I trust to be the in-case-of-emergency contact for me. Now, that says a lot. Thank you, my precious friend, for your steadfast belief in me.

Dearest Karenna Lynn. I believe being present with one who is transitioning from this physical life to the next is a profound gift. And I also feel that having the opportunity to assist, guide, and witness one's intimate transformational journey is equally powerful. Thank you for trusting me with your journey of inner exploration. Your love, Light, and generous support of my work could power the ages.

To my dear friend, Michael Malherek. I have never met anyone with as much personal dedication, drive, and conviction to personal health and well-being as you. Doing whatever it takes for healing and optimal wellness. And all of it with a heaping metaphorical "spoonful of sugar" and the most infectious humor. Thank you for keeping me laughing.

To my brother from a different mother, Paul Isensee. Journeying through life with you, whether near or far, is a valued gift. Your love, support, intellect, and sense of humor are beyond compare. Thank you for always looking out for me and being my buddy.

To my lovely friend and naturopathic doctor, Dr. Pauline Alwes. Thank you, Paula, for your guidance and gracious heart. I could never repay your healing support, kindness, and all the wisdom that you have bestowed. They say your wealth is in your health and you have kept me and Luca oh so rich. I am eternally grateful.

To my wonderful business partners and soul sisters in 5 Points of Light. PK Keiran, Tara Thomas, Janet Granger, and Melissa Majors. Our coming together was destined and magical. Our diversity has amplified our oneness as we see one another in each other. Thank you for the unconditional love and support—you all inspire me.

To the extraordinary Lori Tenny. When we first met, just as I was introducing mindfulness training to the meetings industry, a recognition of a long-overdue reunion was felt. A friendship of lifetimes. Your support of my work and the significance of your contribution in spreading awareness has been invaluable. Thank you, bright light, for everything.

To my friend and composer, Jamie Hosmer, for your gracious support on my first and second meditation CDs *The Temple of All Knowing Chakra Meditation* and *Journey with Guided Meditation*. The ease of creating with you was a delight. Thank you for bringing my words to life with your inspired music.

To my friend and award-winning composer Louis Colaiannia and the incomparable Steve Sundberg of FTM Studios in Lakewood, Colorado for their mind-blowing expertise and generous support on my latest CD tracks for *Storybook Meditations* and the audio program *Connect Your Inner & Outer World Mindfully—Through Chakra Awareness*

& Cleansing. Thank you for helping me share the joy of meditation and inner exploration.

To my wise and beautiful soul sister, Brenda Calvin. Thank you for your Light. We came together through this work many years ago to support humanity. We recognized immediately the depth of our connection that is beyond words and worlds. Thank you!

Dearest Margaret "Mars" Roberts. You are the keeper not only of Rio Sierra Riverhouse, where I wrote my first book and river meditation, but also keeper of the sanctuary. Thank you for your friendship, guidance, generosity, laughter, and love, my sister.

To all the incredible authors of the inspirational quotes contained in this book, I respect and honor you for your courage, your voice, and your dedication to sharing your wisdom. To those who I wanted to include but did not have the real estate to include, I thank you as well because you have touched and guided more souls than you realize. Thank you one and all.

First and last and everything in between, the most potent gratitude I can muster to my Source, Spirit, Principle Substance. And to my team in nonphysical with whom I feel a great kinship—I thank you for your support and credit the wisdom of these pages to all. We are one.

About the Author

Lee Papa is an internationally recognized mindfulness and meditation speaker and trainer. She is highly sought after for her expertise on the topic of well-being from a mindfulness perspective and for her approachable style. She brought mindfulness training to the meetings and events industry with her keynote "How to Live and Lead Mindfully" and her award-winning *Mindfulness Lounge*™.

A frequent contributor to top trade publications and an expert resource for wellness topics, Lee privately supports individual clients through one-on-one coaching, her online programs "Mindful Makeovers" and "A Year of Living MindfulLee," and her audio program *Connect Your Inner & Outer World Mindfully—Through Chakra Awareness & Cleansing*. Her guided meditations can be found on *The Temple of All Knowing Chakra Meditation*, *Journey with Guided Meditation*, and the latest *Storybook Meditation Series* albums. Through these mindfulness-training platforms, Lee is on a mission to support well-being in mind, body, and spirit globally. Visit her at LeePapa.com.